FROM PRIDE

TO LOVE

RANDY STEWART

FIVE STAR
PRESS

TABLE OF CONTENTS

Our lives are inundated with hidden and pronounced expectations which keep us living in fear, of others and what they think. People pleasing and facades plague our responses and we must step outside of self, trusting God in the presence to move forward as His child.

As we let go of the pride of self, we begin to live out love by His grace through His Word and for His glory. The love for our neighbor is evident in our actions as we love as He loved us, knowing that we are forgiven and the courage to accept we are His child by faith.

Why Write This Book?

The information contained in this book is nothing new under the sun. The beauty of what we will discuss is found in simple everyday life. Most of us don't realize how we live out of pride until it is exposed in our lives. Richard Foster writes in his book 'Prayer', that *the point of the teaching is its triviality. Simple, ordinary things are undertaken for the love of God. As we experience the many little deaths of going beyond ourselves, we increasingly enter into the grace of humility. We may think these tiny, trivial activities are hardly worth mentioning. That, of course, is precisely their value. They are unrecognized conquests over selfishness.'*

This brief introduction is written with a contrite pen in hand. To borrow the phrase of Rich Mullins, I am "a mere ragamuffin" who once served on the Navajo Reservation in Arizona for almost seven years as a foster parent and youth pastor, now working with Neighborhood Engagement in Louisville, Kentucky. Our spring and summer work groups on the Reservation became the guinea pigs for a study of this subject that is difficult to confront. God's grace prevailing, though, I would like to share our adventure from pride to love with the goal of a radical self acceptance without self-concern——to be free to live with Jesus as our center.

To find out who we are today, we need to backtrack to the days of yester-year - say middle to high school. As your unique film is being replayed vividly in your mind, you can begin to see the formation of your identity during those years. The 'labels' assigned to you settle in over your head as you penetrate the halls of 'insecurity,' always wondering if you are being noticed by your peers. And the drama lives on, even up to the hour of you reading these words. So hold on tight as we start this journey together out of pride to into love—to something greater than ourselves. We seek to be truly free once and for all to live and love beyond 'me' and 'my' agenda and others' expectations.

The research collected from small group studies on Pride was inspired by Dr. Stuart Scott's book 'The Exemplary Husband'. Far from that title, I realized I needed some work and began to evaluate my life to determine if I live out of "all is me or woe is me." Surprisingly, both realms are dangerous and bring us to a self-focus which manifests itself in pride, leading to a life of either security (all) or insecurity (woe).

INTRO:

ALL IS ME OR WOE IS ME

Either way it's about ME. Dr. Stuart Scott makes an insightful observation about pride in his thirty manifestations of pride when he points out the all powerful "flip side of the coin." We readily observe pride in the context of arrogance, accumulation of material possessions, and pursuit of prestige, status, and wealth. Less obvious, but no less prideful, is my WOE, brought to life by feelings of insecurity and inadequacy. And we discovered from our mission teams that came to the Navajo Reservation that many people fall into the less recognized category of woe.

We suffered (woe) through two to three nights of thirty manifestations from the Pride to Humility chapter in *The Exemplary Husband*. Dr. Scott states that prideful people *'believe that all things should be **from** them, **through** them and to them or for them.'*

Scott writes that *'Self-pitying people desperately **want** to be good, not for the glory of God, but for themselves. They **want** to do things for and by their own power and might for the personal recognition. They **want** everyone to serve them, like them, and approve of them. When these desires are not full-filled, a prideful person will become even more inwardly focused and will continue a vicious cycle.' pg. 5*

As we shared our story and experiences on the Navajo Reservation, multiple groups expressed in handwritten form how they felt pride was affecting their ultimate purpose to live for the glory of God. The stories illuminated dim hearts, and many were liberated and drawn closer to our Savior and His imitation as we let go of self throughout the week. Lord, help us to keep pride in check in our daily schedule, to hourly remove ourselves from our circumstances and into Your love, in response to Your grace that trumps our pride, finding our strength in You.

The responses of our work teams seemed to narrow into three major categories which we will discuss in more detail on our journey from pride to love. We will examine solutions as we begin to evaluate self through the life and example of Jesus. Our conclusion will show us that as we remove self and our pride, His unfailing love will transform our thinking to be others-minded, selfless instead of selfish, and yearning to live for something that is bigger than self as we complete the worship circle.

CHAPTER 1:

PRIDE'S BEGINNING

OUR FIRST THANKSGIVING

I can remember our first Thanksgiving with the Navajo Indians. In great Navajo fashion, our director and Nazarene pastor, James Paddock, stuffed us into his extended cab truck. The kids were relegated to the camper in the very back. We headed northwest to Page to see Lake Powell, where we experienced our first Thanksgiving with the Navajo Indians. Near the Grand Canyon and rated one of the top lakefronts in the United States, Lake Powell was well worth the drive.

I can still visualize that day as one of our first moments on the Navajo Reservation. James' relatives welcomed us to a fresh cattle and sheep butcher for our meat with turkey and more trimmings than Golden Corral. The day is so surreal in my mind as I vividly recall images, ranging from the people to our first encounter with Navajo Tea, which remained unrivaled in all of our seven years on the Rez.

I replay the reel in my mind like it was recorded this morning from one of his relatives. "So how long are you staying?" I guess this was the *first hit to my pride* as I remember the moment so vividly, complete with the defensiveness that struck me on the inside. I explained that our commitment was for one year, but my wife and I realized that to disciple others to Christ would require a longer stay. We enjoyed the rest of our visit and got a hotel room for the night.

The Navajo people were accustomed to people signing up for mandatory two year commitments. They would come and go, but the Navajo people would remain. His question was legitimate in light of his experience. How long will they stay this time?

What length of time is too short or too long? A missionary who had spent 50 years overseas, and whom we visited for counsel before arriving in Arizona, noted that both my wife and I would need a complete peace in our hearts. We had that when we sold our home and left for Arizona. We were not fully ready, but we fully trusted Him through faith.

We drove almost four hours north to see Monument Valley. We actually stayed with a Nazarene pastor who was in *Back to the Future III*, and he had open access to drive us all around and through the mittens. We saw our first traditional male and female hogans, along with amazing views of God's handprints. Our next stop, and another Navajo 'first', was the Canyon of all Canyons, Canyon De Chelly, now a National Monument on Navajo land (ugly sidebar: this is where the U.S. Calvary rounded up the Navajo people and drove them like cattle on the Long Walk. Lord forbid and forgive.)

James drove us through the Canyon during November, which at 6,000 plus feet elevation equates to snow melt and water in the creek up to the middle of your tires. What an adventurous ride as we stopped to climb up to the natural arch in the middle of the canyon that is only accessible by truck. I went up with his twin daughters, Joni and Jodi, and his son, Art. The view really does take your breath away as you sit mesmerized by God's glory and by the reality of how small we are as His children.

It was a moment in life you just don't forget. Though we had many return visits to Canyon De Chelly with work teams and other great experiences, none compared to seeing that Canyon for the very first time with the Paddock family. It is no wonder Rich Mullins also found the presence of God among the Navajo near Window Rock, their capital, where he helped build hogans and worshipped with the Navajo people.

Cookie Jars and Forbidden Fruit

Andrew Murray writes that *"pride made redemption necessary."* The very thing Satan wanted most was to become like God, perhaps even greater, and thus his competition with God and resulting fall from heaven. His pride made redemption necessary for us all, as sin was introduced through Adam and Eve the following drama began to unfold.

We all have a disposition to desire gain. Some motives are pure, and others not so much. We have to travel back in time to see the very first example of B.S. (Blame-Shifting) in **Genesis 3**. You know the story of Adam and Eve, with the forbidden fruit not unlike our off-limit cookie jars of today. The temptation Eve faced had to have been as surreal as that faced by a kid with milk that would go perfectly with a nice cookie. She had a desire for gain, and like a child with milk in hand she saw something pleasing to the eye.

She bites of the forbidden fruit and we steal the cookie, only to try and hide from God… like such a feat is possible. Her response was a model still followed today: she blamed it on the serpent. He made her do it. Then, Adam really got us men in trouble by pointing his finger back to the woman. Thanks, Adam.

At the first sight of controversy or failure, what is the tendency of our human nature? We pull out the oldest pride trick in the book and B.S. (blame shift). "I didn't know," or "He/she was suppose to!'" Can you relate? We really are weak creatures as we try and write things off on someone else's account in a vain effort to uphold our own image. Husbands and executives, do you see the picture now in front of you? "Woman, where are my keys?" "Where did you put them?", or, "Where's my file on the Smith case? Our list of B.S. tricks becomes endless after years of experience in subtlely shifting blame.

The real trouble is that the blame game can deepen to the point of causing real pain. In a recent story from the community, a husband drowning in woe as a result of some of his own choices with alcohol blames his wife for his depression and near suicide. Perhaps the wife didn't stay at home with the kids enough, had to support more of her husband's consumption or "needs", or was married to her work, but that does not give him entitle-ment, born out of arrogance, to blame others for his poor choices. Men and women alike can marry their work or become consumed by other pursuits if balance is not intentionally sought in our lives. May we begin to take responsibility for our actions after we put our hands in the cookie jar or take a bite from the apple.

Judgment Luke 18

Jesus was consistent in reminding us through His parables to not be a Pharisee. As we look at **Luke 18: 9-14,** we learn that "to some who were confident of their own righteousness and looked down on everybody else," Jesus brings the heat. To paraphrase, a Pharisee and a tax collector go up to the temple to pray and the Pharisee has no hesitation placing himself on the main stage, standing up and praying about (or to) himself.

Slow down. *"Or to"* himself, from the footnotes, changes the whole meaning. He is praying, not to God, but to himself. His perception is that

he should be grateful to God for not being like other men whom he ha_
accused, in his own judgment, to be robbers, evildoers and adulterers.
May we all be grateful that Jesus took one of these to paradise from the
cross next to him.

The Pharisee further declares how righteous he is by proclaiming his own
fasting and giving. The tax collector just throws in the towel and doesn't
even get near the guy. Instead, he humbled himself before God, "would
not even look up to heaven," "stood at a distance" and "beat his breast."
The tax collector, not the religious leader, understood his brokenness
before a righteous God. Lord, forgive our mighty towers that we construct
before the One and Only.

MADELINE AND GLORIA

We adopted a widow, Madeline Begay, and her daughter, Gloria, on the
Reservation. We would provide meals, clean-up around their house, and
tend the sheep. They told us a story one day about the judgment they had
experienced from young kids would come out to their property and throw
stones at their house. They knew the ridicule of children and the lonely
feeling of rejection.

THROWING STONES

I can relate to the pain of rejection quite well, and it seems like it was only
a few moments or days ago. Actually, it has been over twenty years now.
The days of high school were so jaded for me, as people would fight to fit
into some group in an effort to belong, ever wandering the halls of insecurity and yearning to be significant or 'cool'. We remember the big
moments in our lives, whether moments of triumph or tragedy, and the rest
become small details that connect our days.

All I can remember was the taunting, mocking and sarcasm that was
hurled from one end of the cafeteria table like a grenade just exploding on
my heart, ever forming the walls of pride as a defense to keep others from
getting too close. What I thought would provide protection only led to
even deeper insecurities. I wasn't exactly the biggest guy in the litter and
was one of the shortest students in our graduating class. I grew in college,
but fell away from God through this pain and my parent's divorce.

13

We wonder why kids are drowning in woe. They feel like they are fighting for their lives. The reality is that hurting people hurt others. It is classic depravity, and we all know the stories of students caught in the middle of the daily drama who have taken their own lives. On an Indian Reservation where suicide rates are higher than average, there is no end in sight and no hope to which to cling. The Navajo people are so desperately in need of encouragement and the love of Jesus. We all are in desperate need of it, regardless of socioeconomic status. We all need His unfailing love.

I'm reminded of the story Jesus tells in **John 8,** where He draws a line in the sand and asks for volunteers from the crowd to throw the first stone at the woman who was caught in adultery. Who walked away first? The older men, out of their wisdom, and then eventually the younger ones lay down their pride and leave the scene. We scoff at that crowd, but how often do we stay behind to throw the stones of judgment?

Moltmann writes that we need to *"accept one another as Christ has accepted you (Rom. 15:7). Only this attitude can give us a new orientation and break through our limitations so that we can spring over our narrow shadows. It opens us up for others as they really are, so that we gain a longing for and an interest in them. As a result of this we become able actually to forget ourselves and to focus on the way Christ has accepted us."*

Despite this powerful insight by Moltmann, what is reality when you meet and "see" someone for the FIRST time? Judgment. Skinny or fat, attractive or ugly, rich or poor, success or failure, prestige or insignificance. What do they do for a living? And then we begin to compete. We think, "I have done that, or have earned this degree also, or live in this area of town too," and the lists go on.

Caveman perception:
Man think: what car have, how big house, in shape or out
Woman think: in shape or out, how many kids, public or private school
Our acceptance or rejection of another person rests on what is external, and we repeat this process everyday.

Becoming a respecter of persons changes our response to that individual. Our expectations of people, along with how they present themselves, influence our thinking. We have not heard their story and do not know the one thing that God does know—their hearts-before we take our seat in the judge's chair. So like Christ, the next time you meet someone, or walk the mall, or - oh yes – even meet a newcomer AT CHURCH, *"become able actually to forget yourself"* and focus on how Christ has accepted you.

Why? For what reason? **In order to bring praise to God according to Romans 15:7.** With a servant's mindset, we realize the worth and value of His creation and we comprehend that in humility we can learn something from every person we come to know.

As you read this story about my friend, Yazzie, watch as my own judgment gives way as new graces emerged in my life, forcing me to rethink my preconceived notions and to show love in acceptance.

Journal 4/08/01   'YAZZIE'S POISON'

I can remember my drive to Phoenix with Yazzie a few months back. He shared about his addiction to alcohol and was honest about his trials. I shared how Christ could help Yazzie overcome his yearning for this drug. Yazzie continued to pray and wanted to meet a local believer to discuss how he overcame his addictions. I believe Yazzie in his heart had communion with Christ and was trusting in Him alone for salvation. I realize Yazzie's struggles, but don't we all struggle with some sin in our life, some area of trial.

If we were honest before God as His children, then we would all admit or should that we are not perfect! Only Christ our Redeemer & Savior was perfect who had no sin in Him! God knows our hearts and the motives behind our choices. I don't believe Yazzie wanted to struggle with alcohol. It just became a physical addiction with his body as he shared that day. His sin just more exposed than perhaps ours.

It is amazing how we Christians even attempt to look so 'ok' on the outside, but inside the scars are there, the pain, the consequence of sin we must live with, past and present. We will all stand before

God and be judged as believers whether done good or bad in the Body of Christ. As a result, let's live for Him in all we do and by our faith be <u>real.</u> Be salty, a light to all those around us that they may see our deeds for His glory and praise our Father in heaven.

BIG BUS ACCEPTANCE AND FOREIGN AID

We return to Madeline and Gloria, the elderly woman and her daughter who had stones thrown at their house. As time went on, we came to love these two women, and Bible stories were exchanged between them and our work groups. I remember junior high students drawing in the sand, telling Madeline about Stephen being stoned to death for his faith and how Jesus was waiting for him in heaven.

What a humble glory to sit at the feet of Jesus in their lives, and hear their story of persecution from our U.S. Calvary and their endurance over the years as they watched their village grow from a trading post to a modern grocery store. I remember the picture well from the day I went to see Madeline just after she celebrated her 90th birthday.

She was sitting in the sheep corral on her feet, just resting with her "children," with the amazing view of buttes and Flagstaff Mountain in the distance. "Feed my sheep," Jesus declares. *Do you really love me?* "Yes, Lord, you know I do." She was the shepherd that loved her flock, and she imparted such grace and humility and love for the Lord. Her contentment in life and joy for what she had and what God had given her in life just radiated from her countenance.

I remember the day the bus pulled in from California. Madeline was getting a new house, and her family had arrived and to do some general clean-up. Faced with more work than they could handle in the short time they had, the family wondered how they would ever clear the ground in time for the approval of the Navajo Housing Authority. A summer work team was serving with the Navajo Christian Foundation and just happened to visit Madeline's house on that particular day. Imagine the family's reaction when out walked about thirty folks from Ceres, California who were ready to clear the land for the foundation of her new home.

16

Madeline and Gloria, along with their family, saw and felt Christ's love that day as compassion and kindness were poured out by His grace. Ordinary people who were strangers just minutes before went to work with open hearts, and the Begay family felt accepted by the Body of Christ. Madeline and Gloria have become a part of our family, and the love He has poured in us has also become unconditional in Madeline's life. What a teaching moment for the work team as they learned first-hand what it means to bring hope in the form of foreign aid. Our short-term work teams were often blessed more than those we went to serve on the Reservation.

The Peace of God continues to be with Madeline and Gloria, and it resonates across the rugged horizon of the Reservation thanks to those who put their faith into action and instilled His hope and Word in others, changing lives for His glory. The stories continue to be told in the sand and we remain teachable in the love and acceptance of the saints.

CHAPTER 2

BROKENNESS AND SELF-CONTROL DRAMA

BROKENNESS

One of the great quotes by **Brennan Manning** is that "to be alive is to be broken and to be broken is to stand in need of grace." In our journey from pride to love, we must stop and realize that we first have to address SELF. Look at Moses and Job, two broken men. God must be able to truly reduce us to nothing before we are able to be used for His glory. The old Puritan prayer says that "vision is found in the valley."

When we remove pride and self and are broken either by a relationship, lack of money or possessions then we have a tendency to slow down and cry out to God for help. It is sad we wait so long, but it is reality in our self-sufficient world. Our souls become alive when we are broken, because in that moment we see how weak we truly are, and we find we are in need of an awesome God who is waiting to extend His hand by grace— to give us something we do not deserve.

Perhaps this is what it means to be poor in spirit, that despite our self-sufficient nature we let go and we trust God. In the broken moments of life we can embrace the truth that His grace is sufficient and we are truly alive only when we are in Him. There is nothing, and no one, else on which to lean in this life.

What was Job's response when he lost everything? Broken, he fell to the ground and worshipped God. He did not curse God. He WORSHIPPED GOD! The Lord gives and takes away, but the name of the Lord is to be praised, **Job 1:21**. Our call in life no matter what we face is to worship God our Father in heaven. However, our focus is often not right or clear. Our tendency is to drown in our own circumstances rather than lift up our heads toward what is unseen. Yes, all of our problems are real and they hurt, but as we remove the veil of self we see with greater clarity the needs of OTHERS. In the valley of brokenness, we fully comprehend the need for a gracious love. So as we see the Greek, Jew, slave or free (**Col. 3:11**) our view of His creation becomes more like that of Christ.

MOMENTS

As time marches on, we find who we are more and more in the everyday moments of life. Sometimes, the moments are bigger – the ones you won't forget. My mom called me recently to tell me that her brother had died. Her parents had already passed and her brother was her only sibling. In the pain of that moment, the feeling hit me that life is closing in. I remembered my childhood, and I was walking through the moments of my own life in the shadow of news that another life had just ended. The moment of a funeral can be surreal like that.

Some moments in life seem to be able to make you or break you, and for strength we have to draw upon a power that is greater than self and what the world sells today. Our world tells us to "Suck it up," the oldest pride response in our history, or "pull yourself up by your bootstraps," depending upon what part of the country you grew up in. In our prideful and self-sufficient human nature, we rarely do anything with the help of our Creator.

Experiencing pain like the loss of a loved one can lead to a real hurt, or even depression, in our lives. We need to embrace the reality of those feelings. Our only chance of overcoming them, though, is not self-reliance, but grabbing the stronghold of the love of Jesus and resting in His arms. Jesus picks us up and brings the living water for life that establishes His love in our hearts.

When we hold on to Him, the power of grace sneaks into our lives. He whispers to us and we find a voice we can trust. Pain gives way to a relationship built on the knowledge that we are loved by God, and we find the peace and joy that surpasses all understanding and comforts us through our moments of trial. The Father is our fortress and refuge in times of trouble. We must remove our pride and self-sufficiency and turn to the only One who can redeem our past and our hurt.

It's no surprise that we make space for God when we hurt, but when the money flows and life is good, we are on autopilot with our lives and focus on self. The poor in spirit remain in a humble and gentle state like Christ, realizing that they depend on Him for their daily bread Blessed are the poor in spirit, for theirs is the Kingdom of Heaven.

Maybe we do become more of an imitation of Christ in the difficult moments. David declared in **Psalm 51:17** that our sacrifice to God is a broken and contrite heart. Our pride is broken by pain. We learn by experience how to humbly love others, because we realize that is what we need, too. Perhaps that is when God works best in our hearts, breaking them for His glory rather than to bring despair. We live out of His power and love, not timidity or fear.(**2 Tim. 1:7**)

We accept His radical love for us, which he offers in spite of our failings, fears, and weak moments, and He raises us up by grace—giving something we do not deserve. We are liberated through the act of submission, which requires us to give Him our burdens and lay down our lives for the Lord. Joy will fill our lives and we really do live poor in spirit because the glory of our responses is for Him and His honor.

By the grace of Christ, we are able to share His love with our neighbors, which includes all who suffer and are broken in their own moments.

HEATHER'S HEALTH

Back in 1997, before coming out to the Rez, Heather had dealt with bad stomach problems from nausea to vomiting. She was getting sick over six times a day during her student teaching days. Everything was fine while she was in high school and college, and "the wreck" occurred in 1995. Heather was hit driving down a country road as a man ran the stop sign resulting in a neck injury. Every gastro test to determine the cause of nausea and vomiting since then has been mysteriously normal.

We went to the Mayo Clinic in Scottsdale, but they were unable to find anything wrong. In the fall of 2005, after almost ten years of suffering, we hit a rough spot. I can remember Elias' birth in October of 2000, and Heather didn't make a sound even without the shot. The doctors were amazed and we gave all praise to God, but one night she came out of the bathroom just crying in pain. Just prior to that episode, she had vomited. We ended up in the emergency room for eight hours, and now we tease that God just wanted us to spend some quiet time together. I called a good friend that night in tears as I hit the floor on my knees, broken and wondering what to do. My friend thought I was joking, because I was having trouble talking through my tears.

All of the tests came back normal, and to this day we wonder about the possibility of her vegas nerve being damaged. The vegas nerve runs from the base of your neck to your stomach. Heather had some whiplash in the wreck, and we couldn't help but wonder if there was some undiscovered nerve damage that was causing her problems. The pain of that time in our lives, and the years of torment for Heather, led us to realize that in suffering we learn obedience. *"...do not be surprised at the painful trial you are suffering, as though something strange were happening to you. But rejoice that you participate in the sufferings of Christ, so that you may be overjoyed when His glory is revealed."* **1 Peter 4:12-13.**

I'll admit I was not overjoyed, but I was humbled and we did learn obedience. We both learned what it means to depend on God, and for that we are grateful. While I only suffered emotionally for Heather, she was in tremendous physical pain. She is a trooper, while at the same time so gentle and patient like Christ. I wonder how she got stuck with a guy like me, but that's God's grace from my perspective. Peter goes on to write that *"we must stand firm in the faith because we know that our brothers throughout the world are undergoing the same kind of sufferings.' And the God of all grace, who called you to His eternal glory in Christ, after you have suffered a little while, will himself restore you and make you strong, firm and steadfast. To Him be the power for ever and ever. Amen."* verses **10-11, Ch.5**

Heather is doing better today. Since that time, we have stepped out in faith and left all we loved and had grown accustomed to with the Navajo, and we moved to Louisville, Kentucky. Heather found an OBGYN in Louisville who recommended the drug Bentyl. Why not? We had nothing to lose by trying it. For ten years we tried every drug known to the gastro world. We give all praise and glory to the Father, for she is now doing well and is stronger today than she has been in the last ten years. We continue to trust God, and He is faithful. We are restored by His grace.

NAVAJOLAND JOURNAL ENTRIES

Journal 9/24/03:   **'DELRAY'**

A few weeks ago one of those times in foster care hit me. This was really the 2nd hardest thing to see or imagine. While watching the kids on the playground Heather gets a phone call from D.E.S. that Delray's mom has died in an auto accident. She had already abandoned the kids but to think of Delray coming home from school excited about a home visit only to find out his mom has passed away.

On the play ground, I looked into the eyes of the other siblings Brianna, Shaylnn and Darwin. I could not imagine losing my mom to death at around five to seven years of age. Delray is seven. He will probably be the only one that really remembers his mom. That night I went home and began playing the 'tar' as Elias, my son, first coined the phrase. At first, I began to pick around on the guitar and found a cool sound, then recalled 'Famous One' by Chris Tomlin and began to strum. The first song written was 'Sweet Embrace' for Delray.

It hurts the heart to think of this boy's loss. There is a deep wound now left by not only the death of his mom, but remaining in foster care away from his family after the loss. Lord, please comfort these children and help me be a light of love to Delray as we both together 'run to your arms open wide'. I love you Jesus!

FROG HAIR AND DAVID'S HUG

I got a phone call to join a foursome for a golf outing. I enjoy the challenge of the game. One good shot is enough to bring you back to the course. The cause was unknown until we arrived at the outing. The event was for Applepatch, an organization that helps mentally handicapped people find assistance through hospice and housing, near Louisville, the base of our mobilization ministry.

As we started our day we were off to a bad start to say the least, barely shooting par and moaning over missed opportunities. The great fellowship took a back seat to our focus on the score. I did happen to hit a great nine iron 125 yards with the ball landing two inches from the hole for a birdie putt. Apparently I was the only one who thought it was a nice shot. The competitive nature was alive, but no worries. "Keep swinging," I told myself.

As the day rolled on, we come upon a hole where a volunteer sat with a mentally handicapped man in 80 plus degree weather, seemingly waiting for us to come upon the frog hair to hit our ever so important birdie or bogey putt. Applepatch is dedicated to building homes in a community for mentally handicapped adults in an effort to provide encouragement and love.

As we approached the green, David got out of his chair with some high ankle strap type boots. He was elated as he told us about the four eagle putts he had made during the day, and then he tapped one of our team's balls in for his fifth. He was so full of excitement and gave us a high five. I remember the surreal moment as he pulled us in and gave us a hug. He was so carefree and full of unconditional love.

I then wondered about my ability to accept others. When was the last time I just shook a stranger's hand and took them in for the hug the first time I met them? It has only happened to me one other time in my life when I met a new youth pastor while out on the Navajo Reservation. We walked away from that green changed, if only for a moment. I was silent after that hug, and allowed God to slow me down and examined my priorities. How blessed we are to have our mental capacity to learn, communicate, work hard and share the love of Christ with those in need.

Four men walked away humbled by David's hug that day. It made the outing worth the frustration of our scores. He displayed so much joy just to be with us and serve us by tapping in our putt. Lord, crash through our wall of pride to allow us to see great importance in the small things, in the mundane, when no one is looking. Help us accept the sweet embrace of a young man with joy. How slow our own mind is if we don't see this as something beautiful to Jesus. He is all and in all for His glory, **Colossians 3:11**.

BEING TAKEN IN STOLEN GOODS AND TRUSTING GOD

At first, I thought I was going crazy when I lost some cash. Maybe I just misplaced it, or forgot that I moved it to another location in the house. But then Heather found some pens in one of the foster boys' pants pockets. So she confronted the boys one day as they returned home from school. It made for a tense situation for the guilty party. Although I was angry to some degree, my concern was the mystery of what was happening in their hearts. What had we done to the boys, or not done for them, that led them to make these poor decisions? You have to hear their story to find the answer. This is where we so often fail in the church, believing our own preconceived notions before we ask any questions.

Can you imagine this just for a moment? The boys lost their dad at age ten. Then, they didn't see their mom for four years. She was out on the streets of Phoenix and gave two older siblings up for adoption before these two ended up in foster care. If that wasn't enough, they were placed with an aunt who physically abused them before they came to our home.

How would that affect you? They had no new reports from their case-worker and had been in the children's home for four months without a chance to visit any of their family members. These boys were hurting from an open wound in their heart, and this was their way of acting out in an attempt to fill the void. We need to slow down, ask questions, and learn a person's story before we dismiss them because of their actions. Otherwise, where are forgiveness and grace to be found? Yes, we need to be discerning, and there is a place for Christ-like rebuke and discipline. But we could often use more patience in our response to situations like this.

Discipline was the hard part in this story, knowing the boys' backgrounds. The guilty party did however work off the debt for the missing items. But that wasn't the end of the story for Heather and me. The time of dealing with the stolen items was hard, and it lingered for us. It was a stressful season wondering what was around the next corner.

The Lord spoke to my heart one night while I was preparing a lesson for a youth event. *"Trust in me, son,"* He seemed to say. "Be encouraged, for I am with you and worthy of praise." As I sat there, I looked up at the wall where a blanket hung, full of verses we had been given by our church. I was encouraged by the Body of Christ in that moment.

I began to remember the calling and the miracles that got us to Arizona. How the Lord blessed us indeed as we trusted in Him with all of our hearts and leaned not on our own understanding. The trial was new, but the moment passed away in our lives and we learned and grew through Him and the endurance and encouragement of the Scriptures, as **Romans 15:4** says.

I thanked God that day for the time of reflection, and I wrote in my journal that I give all thanks to God for my wife, my son Elias, and His love! I sense His grace displayed in our life. He has blessed us beyond measure, and I pray that His blessings will continue on Elias, that he might be great in the Lord's sight like John the Baptist. I believe God has answered that prayer just by his birth. My prayer was for one family, one heritage, Lord and baptism, serving Him with no divorces or splits and honoring the King for His glory. I praised the Lord in 2001 and I continue to praise Him now for His unconditional love and support, even in difficult times. It is the strength that only comes from Christ.

LAKE POWELL, RAINBOW BRIDGE AND SELF-CONTROL ISSUES

The men's retreat on the Rez rolled around again in the summer of 2002, and Heather and Elias flew back home to see her family. My intern and I headed out to Lake Powell in the heat of the summer in an old 1991 Jeep with no air conditioning. I still don't know what were we thinking, although at least we were going to a lake where we could swim and cliff jump.

The weekend began with the Jeep dying at a stoplight in Flagstaff. I was just dreading the thought of being stranded between Flagstaff and Lake Powell, which was about two hours away. But we finally made it safely to the Lake and camped out before a bridge that was near a trucker's stop off the road. The sleeping arrangements consisted of hard red rock. Needless to say, we were up at 5:00 a.m. to check in at the Visitor Center and find a four wheel off road trail.

The road led to the North side of the lake. We got stuck in the sand a time or two, but four-low got us out and on to our swimming cove. It was hot to say the least, and we swam across the lake to a landing and hiked over to another beachfront. I watched my younger counterpart swim like an Olympian while I tried to hide the fact that I was perpetually out of breath. We found a small twenty-foot jump off the rocks , and afterwards we were so ready to eat a decent meal.

We ended up at Denny's of all places, and we took a few minutes just to soak up some much needed air-conditioning. We called the boat rental to secure and verify our voyage. But at the last minute I saw a brochure with cheaper prices equating to a hundred dollar difference, so we took the bait. I know now that you should never change your plans at the last minute, especially when you have to load and unload the boat yourself.

WINDTALKERS AND REMEMBERING THE NAVAJO

After Denny's we headed out for an evening in Page, Arizona, and decided to see the movie *Windtalkers*, about how the Army used the Navajo language to code messages so the Japanese could not figure out their operations. The movie itself brought out many emotions from our time with the Navajo. The stereotypical Hollywood shots of Monument Valley were in full color, and while Canyon De Chelly scenes would have been nice, we were at least grateful for the story being told.

We headed out to the parking lot and got back in the Jeep with the high hopes of better sleeping arrangements. But the engine would not start. I was already upset after spending the previous couple of hours processing the story of the Navajo code talkers in between apparent racist remarks from other people inside the theatre. Now I had to deal with the Jeep. And in the middle of it all I was missing Heather and Elias. It was enough to cause me to weep. We took a moment to pray, and the Jeep eventually started. We were so tired that we just found a place to park in a local park to catch a few hours of sleep.

SELF-CONTROL: A FRUIT OF THE SPIRIT?

The next day we got the boat, a twenty-seven foot cruiser with a cabin down below. It was the same price as a smaller version. We unloaded the boat without incident, and I decided to take the boat out for a little spin while the truck was being returned. I immediately lost the float off the sides, but I was able to quickly retrieved it. It was only the first mishap in what was to become a very long day.

We headed out on Lake Powell, destination Rainbow Bridge, one of the largest natural rock covered bridges in the United States. It was forty-five to fifty miles from our launch site. I had trouble parking the boat near the pier since I was used to the brakes of a car. Others began watching and I could just feel the hairs rising off the back of my neck. But I managed. We walked down to see Rainbow Bridge. It was grandiose, but the moment was short as we just took some pics and headed back toward a beachfront.

We found a sweet forty to fifty foot jump to climb up by the edge of the lake and we hoisted the anchor from the boat. The boat began to drift toward the rocks and I had to keep circling so we could attempt this enticing cliff jump. We ended up relaxing and swimming around by the boat. We wanted to be sure to have the boat back by 6:00 p.m., so we decided to begin the 15-mile journey back towards the launch site where we began. That's when we discovered that the engine would not start! We gave it some gas to try to start it, but then I remembered the guy at the marina said not to do that. We waited another hour, and then the wind picked up and pushed us towards the rocks. I had no trouble envisioning scratch marks up and down the side of the boat. I did have trouble seeing how we would pay for it.

Our intern quickly went past anger to near lack of self-control. His leg became entangled in the anchor rope and he frantically tried to get out of the mess by twisting and hurling razor sharp sarcasm like flaming arrows. I was laughing on the inside, but also tried to retain control and patience. I had to force myself to forget that we were stuck in the middle of Lake Powell with no clue what to do.

Finally, some guys who clearly did not expect to run into a breathalyzer test on the Lake stopped to help. They gave the boat some gas and it

29

started as we watched in disbelief. After learning some new vocabulary from our new friends, we noticed that the time was 4:00pm and we had to have the boat back by six. We took off toward the marina, eager to get back in time and with the boat in one piece.

We arrived at the marina with plenty of time, and I cleaned out the boat and loaded out stuff back in the truck. The situation seemed to have returned to good order. As I rode in the back of the truck, I heard a man cry out that we were scraping bottom. I yelled at the truck to STOP, STOP! But it was already too late. Two props were toast.

We got the boat back to the office, and walked out with six hundred and fifty dollars less than what we took in. The next time you rent a boat all day, get the $35 insurance that would have covered this mess. In the end, yes we had fun. But we also lost the fruit of the Spirit at times, or to take from **Romans 3:23,** we fell short of the glory of God." We learned a valuable lesson that day with elements of impatience, anger, fits of rage and self-control power outages that reminded us of our need to slow down, pray and rely on the Father. Where was my faith?

At our worst moment when the boat would not start in the Bermuda Triangle of Lake Powell, all I could remember was my wife's example of patience and how I knew I had to have a right response with my intern. He was boiling over, but I had to remain calm, if only on the outside, if we were to gather any resolve in the midst of our situation. I thank the Lord for Heather's example of love and patience, especially with Elias. Praise be to God for her life. She is a blessing to me and our son. She is my better half that keeps the boat from sinking in the midst of storm.

CHAPTER 3:

POSSESSIONS, IMPATIENCE AND ANGER

MANIFESTATIONS OF PRIDE

TIGHT GRIPPED GREENBACKS

This is a subject nobody wants to talk about out loud unless it involves how to make more on this or that investment. We rarely hear about giving from the heart when we know some person is in need, even if they are a loved one or close relative. The average American is so consumed by wealth or their pursuit of it. We work and fight for more when contentment is great gain.

But this is not how the world measures success. Instead, our scales seem to be square footage, Beamers and Benzos. We place our hope in ourselves and our monetary worth, rather than our identity as a child of God. His Word tells us to "not be arrogant or to put our hope in wealth which is so uncertain." Think about our society's reaction to a stock market crash. Compare that with the knowledge that God has no crashes. We have been called to be generous, willing to share, and rich in good deeds from **2 Timothy Ch. 6**. Through that, we take hold of the life that is truly life.

John Piper has hit the nail again on this subject in ***Desiring God***. He writes, *"The reason the use of your money provides a good foundation for eternal life is not that generosity earns eternal life, but that it shows where your heart is. Generosity confirms that our hope is in God, and not in ourselves or our money. We don't earn eternal life. It is a gift of grace (**2 Tim. 1:9**). We receive it by resting in God's promise. <u>Then how we use our money confirms or denies the reality of that rest.</u>"*

Whew! Piper convicts us all in the USE of our resources. As believers, are we throwing in both coins, like the woman Jesus notes in Luke? Some give from their wealth. The poor woman gave all she had. It wasn't the size of the gift, but the size of her heart.

May God help us in this tight gripped battle to let go of what is rightfully His, given to us by grace. May we live content, able to use our wealth to bless others who are in need. Our affluence as Americans is one of our main sources of pride. Still, we feed it everyday as we place tiny idols of possession before joy in God and His greatness and majesty. Lord, forgive our pride.

How often must God laugh from on high at our shuttle launches, air shows and skyscrapers, when He holds the universe in balance? In our human pride and arrogance pray our politicians don't ever remove In God We Trust from our currency. Do we really? In God We Trust, or the physical greenback itself? Loosen your grip!

MY HANDS: GIFT OR GIVER

It seems as we work up the social/church/corporate/golden ladder we have this sense of ownership and pride of possession. We have earned or worked hard and deserve nice things, and in our natural depravity our inclination is to declare that our hands have made this thing or bought this object. The problem is that our love and worship is of the gift and not the Giver, as **Deuteronomy** says, "You may say to yourself, 'My power and the strength of my hands have produced this wealth for me. But remember the Lord your God, for it is He who gives you the ability to produce wealth." **Ch. 8, verses 17-18**.

We have to be careful or the worship of the gift will become our affection, and all the toys can become false gods - substitutes for the Giver of Life eternal. We must remember that our power and strength comes from the One and Only who holds all things together and, like Uzziah, the pride of our little kingdoms will be our downfall.

Give your love and affection to the Giver of the gifts. Thank you God, Jesus and Holy Spirit, for your gifts. May we never let them replace You.

SARCASTIC BIRTH OF IMPATIENT ANGER

One of the largest categories of pride manifestations, as polled from our work groups on the Rez, begins with sarcasm. It is so easy for sarcasm to turn in to anger. One college student noted that sarcasm is essentially a "socially acceptable way of not liking someone." Sarcasm helps us break the ice, or 'tease' and test the dynamics of a new group. But it can become bothersome, and may even end up hurting another member on the team. What is intended as light-hearted banter can balloon over time, and the

33

object of the sarcasm can be deeply affected.

A girl on one of our work teams was really concerned about the group's continued use of sarcasm to either bring someone else down or elevate themselves in the course of conversation. As we went through the various manifestations of pride, she just broke down and wept about how it made her feel. I would add here that most arrows thrown are pulled from the deep baggage of insecurity. The intent may be to hurt others or to bring others to the same competitive level as we find ourselves. Someone might hit a homerun unless we keep them in check. This is even more sad when it is found within the Church. Paul tells us in Galatians to especially do good to fellow believers, and yet in this American land of competition we feel the need to slay the giant with a few sarcastic stones. Regardless of the old tune, words really do hurt us.

Think of the reaction or your spouse or significant other if you say, "Did you know the gym is open late until 10pm?" No need to translate that one. Or what about your reaction to a co-worker who says, "Power go out last night and you didn't reset your alarm clock?" translated, "man you show up late every time I have something important to present." The list goes on with simple "comments," which might create some laughter in new settings, but also have the potential to hurt others. Remember **Ephesians 4:29**, which reminds us, "…to not let any unwholesome talk come out of our mouths but only what is helpful for building others up…"

IMPATIENCE: The First Placement and Blessing and Woe

We moved from the frozen tundra of the Midwest to the Arizona desert. At an elevation of 6,000 feet, the desert is mild during the day but below freezing at night during the winter. Our family from back home visited us on for our first Christmas day on the Rez. The day had a high of 55 degrees, and we hiked out on one of the buttes. The thought that we would soon be foster parents was heavy on our minds that holiday season. The unknown is what we feared most, but the foster care training and preparation was exciting at the same time. We learned to trust the mystery of God's hand.

As the New Year of 2000 came around the corner our hearts were ready for children, if not our minds. The body is weak, but the spirit is willing. But we soon found out we were not so ready for young ones. Ready or not, the day finally arrived. No amount of training could have prepared us for our first placement of Navajo children.

The childrens' case worker called us at around 2:30 one afternoon to have us join her and our first placement of children. We walked in her office and she had blessed four children with popcorn, which seemed like a reasonable act of kindness. The reasonableness of the decision began to fade when the kids began spilling kernels all over the floor. We made our first attempt at discipline in a cross-cultural context. Exactly. Not happening.

The kids began throwing the popcorn at us, and we wondered, "Lord, what have you called us to out here in the desert?" as the case worker seemed oblivious to the kids' behavior. The oldest, Shawna, was around 11, Dale was 9, Brad was 5, and Brian was 4. This was real life. The adventure continued at home as Brad would simply not respond to discipline. He often stuck his tongue out at us and was always the defiant one. The older two just coped and the youngest was happy to have attention, but Brad was the real test.

BLESSINGS COME IN SMALL PACKAGES

Amazingly though, after two weeks of consistent and loving discipline, Brad would stop and listen to our instruction. Then, I found what impatience looked like. Or I should say, Blessing. She was placed in our home as a 16 month old severely neglected infant. She had an open sore under her chin, bad diaper rash, and an ear infection. At the same time. Today we have a seven year old son, and an ear infection alone is near death. This poor baby had that plus more. She literally cried in pain all day with 15 to 20 minute breaks of being pleased by either a meal or some toy.

It was one of the hardest times my wife and I have experienced in foster care. Endurance is key with four children, a pregnant wife who was rethinking child birth all together, and poor little Blessing in so much pain even while on medication. Or was it poor me? You see, I was watching 'my' comfortable little pre-Rez world, which included being married with no children, come crashing down, and yet our intent was to serve others and be His example.

Instead, all I can remember is how impatient I became with Heather, the kids and even Blessing. It was hard taking all this in and yet something was shouting in my heart - persevere and love.

Blessing left after two weeks and was placed with her grandma instead of her young teenage Navajo parents. The other four children also left our home and were reunited with their parents, who started attending a local church. We actually attended the parents' wedding.

Our Hogan was empty again as our life seemed to settle on the Rez, and we awaited more children. The phone rang after some rest following the previous placement, and the person on the other end asked if we would take in a young 2 year old girl. I wondered,,do we know the family? Turns out, it was Blessing!

We gasped and just looked at each other that day, and we realized that God was giving us one more chance to love her with His heart and patience. She was absolutely a changed girl after six months and was so playful and full of joy. My wife is so patient, but I knew I had failed in some way and wanted to make it right. I wanted to be His imitation, and I realized that would require a dose of humility.

God taught me through that experience that we learn how selfish we are when we see ourselves from the perspective of a child. I pray for many men and dads now that they will slow down and really see, absorb and listen to their children. I can still be guilty now of not sitting at the feet of Jesus with my son. Christ alone is our strength when we are pushed to the edge. We need to take a step back. Put the Blackberry or iPhone down, and go hold your loved ones.

ANGER MICRO-MANAGEMENT

The pest of general irritability or impatience leads us to our next major downfall in pride that leads to arrogance displayed in anger. Our assumption in our self-focused world when some expectation of ours has not been met is that we have a right to be angry. Frustration from unrealized expectations so dictates our world because we set this 'silent bar' as if people should read our minds and knowingly meet our demands.

I have been doing some outreach with an inner city ministry, and a volunteer told me he had been reading a book by a Jewish rabbi that says our arrogance creates our response of anger. It appears that this sense of entitlement grows up out of our arrogance. Do we have rights? The King of Kings, our Savior, had every right, and yet in his greatest trial Isaiah tells us he remained silent like sheep before a shearer.

Perhaps in our arrogance as we flirt with the idols of prestige and honor, we would do well to slow down and remember to be sheared first by the Father. The pruning of our hearts that comes from the Word steers us to humility and gentleness in our responses. Without it, our impatient attitudes that breed anger can be devastating. Our entitlement becomes another person's guilt trip, all because they failed to show us the respect we deserve or meet our needs. God, help us to hear your Word from **Proverbs 15:1** that a gentle answer turns away wrath, but a harsh word stirs up anger.

DEAD TO SELF AND THE PATIENT MAN

"The fact that many things often displease and disturb you is because you are not perfectly dead to yourself, nor have you cut yourself off from the things of this world."— Imitation of Christ, by Thomas a' Kempis (p. 49)

How true this quote from a' Kempis is, if we take a close look at ourselves. We are so focused on the outside and external things, and we become hurt and offended by the slightest comment or criticism. We seek consolation, not from God and His Word, but from the creatures of this world. Those creatures can be prestige, entitlement, respect or public opinion. We are not really dead to self until we stop looking around and start looking up.

a' Kempis goes on to write, "I cannot bear such an action coming from such a man, nor do I have to put up with it. He has seriously wounded me, charging me with things I never would have dreamed." (pg. 102).
The truly dead to self man though will accept trials and not just from

people of his choosing, but with new graces emerging over our pride, respond like Jesus. Whomever hurts you by words or accusation must still be loved and forgiven as we walk like Christ becoming the patient man.

We have to learn to let go of self. Then, we can embrace the trials that are before us, however significant, because they become light and momentary when our focus is shifted from the temporal to the eternal. And as we let go of self, our hands are free to grab the stronghold of His sufficient grace.

As the scales of pride fall away and the light of Christ is revealed in us, our natural reaction to life's curves begins to resemble the imitation of Jesus.

CONTROL ISSUES:

I can remember the good ole (kid) days of dad exercising way too much control. He would yell to 'turn your light off' as he walks by my room while I am downstairs watching television. All he had to do was flip the switch. The issues only become bigger as we grow up, like our decisions about who to date and which college to attend, and the child's perception of a parent's control is no different.

I find myself now trying to exercise control over small things in my own son's life, and it makes me wonder, when does the control cycle ever end? Or, in our pride, does it continue indefinitely? We want to control the inputs and outputs of our own lives, as well as the lives of others, in order to achieve whatever end result we desire.

Where is our trust in God when we control and manipulate our situations and the people around us? We do this inadvertently sometimes, like offering to buy dinner or pay for some other item.

I have a finance background, but then Jesus wrestled control of my spread-sheet away from me. I have made progress in letting go, but still struggle sometimes. Decreasing our control over own lives will require, and also produce, an increase in our faith and our ability to trust God. The more we let go of self and actually obtain that last fruit of the spirit, the self-control to refrain from exercising control, the more we can enjoy rest in the wonder of His desires.

A WALK THROUGH THE NARROWS

I remember our preparation for the daunting task of the "Narrows", a swift river bed surrounded by canyon walls at Zion National Park in Utah. For almost the first five miles upstream, the terrain consisted of slippery rocks covered with algae. We were in a fierce warrior moment carving out our walking sticks that we hoped would help us maneuver the current and keep our balance. Some had crosses and Scripture written on them, complete with burn marks and rope attached. We were such amateurs.

It took us almost three hours to casually hike to the Big Spring, which was no Havasu Falls, a waterfall at the base of the Grand Canyon, but a great view nonetheless and new adventure. We swam for a few minutes in the cold water, in and out of the shade along the trail. On the way out we decided to have our own amazing race. I got trapped at one point on the rocks because I could not jump in the water with my camera. I lost some ground, but quickly caught up, all the while slipping like crazy on the algae covered rock.

ROCKY THE SQUIRREL

By God's grace we made it out in less than an hour and ten minutes, not bad for five miles of rough terrain. We were tired and beat down, and our legs were mush. We were as hungry as the squirrels that were running nearby looking for something to eat, so we sat down on a ledge and began to open up our packs. We were ready to devour anything in sight, and we had some furry friends accompany us at our feet.

One squirrel we'll name Rocky came up to my feet, and with both of his little paws reached out and took a chip from me and ate it with no hesitation, scurrying along to the next handout. We captured some video footage of me actually petting the back of his little head while he munched on some righteous grub. This was like Looney Tune heaven or some cartoon moment you yearn for as a child, just chilling with God's creatures.

LAKE POWELL RETURNS AND ANTELOPE POINT

Our journey continued to Lake Powell for some swimming and relaxation, but once again the serene lake quickly turned to frustration. We got a room during the day because one member of our team was feeling sick and decided to stay back while the rest of us set out on an unchartered mysterious trek to some cove on the lake. Smart move on his part, not so much on ours.

We headed out in the blazing and dry heat of Page, Arizona, in the middle of the day when it was around 104 degrees. Some brush scratched up the SUV while we were driving back to the cove from the main road. We had trouble finding our destination, which was supposed to take us right up to the water. Meanwhile, the battery indicator showed that the vehicle's battery was close to dying and we grew nervous about the prospect of being stuck out in the middle of the desert without much water. So we decided to retreat back to the motel for some rest and then off to another point on the lake.

Antelope Point was a new adventure for us, and one where we enjoyed some great forty foot jumps. Soon, the hour for us to leave the lake was upon us. And you guessed right... no battery. The vehicle was dead, We were on the lookout for a little divine deliverance.

When a guy did stop and offer help, our first response was, "We're not worthy." But we were able to send someone to Wal-Mart for a new battery. The next morning we took the SUV to a mechanic for the alternator to be fixed, and we were ready to return home. But it wasn't time for us to get home yet. We managed to run out of gas a few miles outside of Flagstaff, and once again we were forced to rely on the help and compassion of a passerby.

I was reading in **Matthew** about how Jesus healed the crowd and saw their need for hunger. He expressed His desire to have compassion on these people. Without food, they might have collapsed on their journey. Jesus met their physical need in that situation, and they were satisfied. He was right there in front of the need, and He took action to meet it. How often do we keep driving and pretend that the homeless are invisible to us?

What *fear* prevents us from reaching out to those right in front of us to meet even their most basic needs?

Discernment is needed, but so is compassion inspired by the example of Christ. God, help the Church to accept the condition of other people in spite of the real trauma or sheer pride that has left them on the streets or on the side of the road. May we be His imitation and may we allow Him to open our eyes and remove our pride. Thank God that He is sovereign, and that He still uses the remnants of the broken loaves to nourish undeserving hearts.

CHAPTER 4

LISTEN AND LEARN: FROM GOD AND OTHERS

REVIVAL TENTS AND THE CROSS CULTURAL IMMERSION

Walking out of our crystal cathedrals with stained glass windows, it's hard to mentally step into a tent, but this is an important stretch of our journey from pride to love. We held a revival on the Rez, and the first night was hard to understand. The speaker was Emery Long from Farmington, New Mexico. His presentation was solidly from God's Word with some surprise as you expect more emotionalism from the sermon at a revival. It's good to lay down the expectations in our pride of preconceived notions with a willingness to learn.

Long spoke of how we needed to not only hear the Word, but we need to read and then study, meditate and memorize God's Word. At the revival, a great woman of faith who planted churches on the Reservation and was in ministry for over forty years thanked Heather and I for coming to her land to help the children and her people. Her name was Florence Yazzie.

Florence also interpreted many songs for the Navajo Hymnal and later became a great friend and sister in Christ. At her funeral which we sadly missed while in Indiana speaking for the mission, we were noted as honorary pallbearers. She was the imitation of Christ, patient, loving and faithful to our Father by word and deed.

Upon our arrival on the Rez, we learned that the Navajo shake hands with everyone else when they get together in church. This was a new experience, not to mention a germ magnet waiting to attract various coughs amidst the congregation. I'm not a germ phoebe, but I could sense the dismay from some of our work groups who had the hand pump sanitizer on demand. I jest, but it is great to shake hands and connect with people through that custom. It is amazing how something so simple can communicate such great respect for those around us.

James asked me to pray at the end of the last night of the revival. I was waiting for another brother named Randy to come forward and pray for the church. But he was talking to me, and I was humbled that night to have such an opportunity. God used the Holy Spirit that night to move hearts as one couple shared how they appreciated the prayer. It really was not me, but God guided my heart to tell His story.

COMMUNION AND FELLOWSHIP

On the last night of the revival, we had our first communion with the Navajo. It was a blessing to focus on Jesus' sacrifice with our new family. James' wife Carol even hugged us both, which refreshed our hearts. James' asking me to pray was a first step in breaking some of my pride, as he accepted me and introduced me to his people. James often jokes that the NIV is the "Navajo Indian Version" of the Bible. He told his congregation, "If you are wondering why these white people are here, it is to give the church some color." Joking aside, James has been very gracious with us.

There were many more nights under the starlit skies, with great fellowship at Navajo revivals and with our hearts beating in one accord all for the glory due Jesus' name.

OPEN RANGE FOR VACATION BIBLE SCHOOL

A work team from Ohio came out and put on a Bible school program at Indian Wells, a community ten miles from Dilkon, and the evening literally became a riot. As we were teaching the lesson curbside, the kids suddenly took off running and bolted toward some cows that were passing through the nearby housing area. Right in the middle of "God so loved the world," they were off like rabbits. One kid was carrying a lasso, which we assumed was for the cows.

After chasing the cows for a few moments the kids turned back to our group. It was then that lasso king decided to rope a kid and bring him to the ground by his ankles. Boom! The coordinator of the work group, known now as Castanza paid lasso king seventy-five cents to rope one of the girls. The seventy-five cents was probably not necessary. The poor girl was lassoed around the neck, and we had to come to her rescue. But then, it was time for revenge.

The lasso 'boy wonder' had some talent, and he next roped Castanza around the arms. He pulled so tight that visible marks were left on Castanza's flesh. Lasso king's posse joined to bring in the kill, while Castanza yelled for help as he was being dragged across the lawn. The rope burns served as a constant reminder of Castanza's love for Christ, as well as the beauty of God's creation displayed in the Navajo children. It was a riot! The outreach opportunity that day was incredible. We got to know the kids by name, and we shared the love of Christ by choosing not to brand the lasso king.

EAR WAX TO SELECTIVE MEMORY

This is a wake up call to all the men out there who do not take seriously the dreaded question, "Did you hear what I just said?" I am speaking to myself also, as our pride as men sometimes does not give way when it comes to REALLY LISTENING to our family. Not just hearing their voices like a radio or television in the distant living room.

We come home from work frazzled by the day's burdens and your girl-friend, wife or kids are ready to share their day. But it just hits the wax and bounces back. In your mind you think, "what was that?" We are not in tune with their day, but still absorbed in our own world. Our focus on self and our own tiredness only allows us to retain selective events, mostly those that directly apply to our own situation. So, if what my wife just told me involves my responsibility to action and time then I hear her. But if it's about her time schedule, telling me her plans, 'oh yes, okay, yea that sounds great' and then we think thirty seconds later 'what did she just say'.

Guilty men? If not, good job. You can move on to the next chapter. For those still reading, we have got to slow down, sit down, and just BE with our family. Our spouse and kids so want our attention, yet we miss the boat in our pride ship that is full of more important items on our agenda. We become so inward focused, and this breeds impatience with those around us.

Truly caring for others' needs and their lives is only possible when we slow down and LISTEN to others. It requires changing our mindset to that of a servant, even when we are tired.

So for all of us, women included now, may we listen to one another with a deep concern about others' burdens. May we learn how to pray with intention and focus. Listening to the hearts of other people and removing our own ambition will free us, if just for a moment, from pride and enable us to embrace the people God places in our lives.

THE FAST SLOW DOWN

God has really spoken to my heart during times of fasting. Removing self from my mind, and remembering the needs of others, requires a conscious choice. Withholding food from the body during a fast shows us we don't need much to survive. Although I sometimes wonder how I will ever make it to the next meal. It is amazing how we can be programmed by our culture to think we need something to have real life.

The fast acts like a pause button on life, and new graces emerge during a time of intense focus and prayer. The little things we often think are important seem to fade away in our weakness, because we learn to lean on God instead of our own false assurances. Priorities change when we see life through His eyes, and fasting has a way of bringing His perspective into sharper focus. We remember others' needs and prayer requests, and we earnestly take them before God during the fast.

Some people question the importance or effectiveness of fasting. The best reason to fast is to follow Christ, who modeled fasting for us. If you have serious decisions to make in your life, then I would urge you to find the answers in the fast.

Another benefit of fasting is that it forces us to listen. Think of **James 1:19,** where we are instructed to be quick to listen, slow to speak and slow to anger. Our natural tendency is to do just the opposite. We are so ready to defend our position or share our opinion on an issue. Perhaps we need to hear a person's story and listen to others' hearts before we cast our reel of knowledge upon them. Bonhoeffer writes the following in *Life Together*:

> "Christians, especially ministers, so often think they must always contribute something when they are in the company of others, that this is the one service they have to render. They forget that listening can be a greater service than speaking."

Bonhoeffer also writes:
> "It is an impatient, inattentive listening, that despises the brother and is only waiting for a chance to speak and thus get rid of the other person…here too our attitude toward our brother only reflects our relationship to God."

Ouch. He just had to add that last part about our relationship with God, linking it with our attitude. But he's right. In our pride, we always seem to be in a hurry. May we use the tool of the fast to imitate Christ, appreciate the value of others, and renew our patience so that we can respond to others and their needs as Christ would.

SHOPPING FOR BOOKSTORE NUGGETS

The greatest leadership advice I have received in some time came in the oddest form at a Barnes & Noble bookstore. I picked up a book in the politics section about Jimmy Carter's life. As I began to peruse this book a story a nugget emerged that was given to President Carter in regard to leadership.

President Carter asked a Mexican leader for his greatest advice. The leader of Mexico responded, "To Love God with everything you have with your heart, mind, soul and strength. And secondly, love the person standing right in front of you."

Think about the last conversation you had with a person who was right in front of you. Were you really listening, engaged in this person's life, worries and burdens? Did you see only what was in front of you, or did you see the *potential* that God placed in this person's life? Maybe you were thinking about lunch, being late for a meeting, or who was going to pick up your kids the next day.

Next time, take the time to listen to the person standing right in front of you. Love the person God puts right in front of you and listen to their story. God places people in your path for a reason. So remove your own selfishness and pride, forget about your time and to do list, and love unconditionally like Christ. Treat that person the way you would want to be treated.

LILLIAN AND EDWARD'S

SUNFLOWER BUTTE

The road to Sunflower Butte, and the home of Lillian and Edward, was four or five miles long, and full of thick washboard bumps. Lillian and Edward are two amazing elders of the church who have walked with the Lord for many years. Our bodies bounced up and down in the car, and the secret was to drive at around 40 miles per hour – faster than your intuition would suggest – to glide over the bumps.

The work team from Ceres, California finally made it out to the couple's home at Sunflower Butte. The butte towers into the sky with a flat top formation at the crest, and it is quite a leery climb. I can remember my first journey up the butte with Lillian's grandchildren and our quest to find an eagle's nest. My wife was pregnant at the time with our first child and my only prayer was to make it off the sheer cliff edge that was part of our path to this nest. The Hopi like to come onto Navajoland and steal the eagle eggs for their ceremonies.

At the top of the butte you can see down to an old ruin site with three circles of stone that once acted as a campsite on a flat landing. Pottery shards are scattered around, and it is fun to take in the history of the land, the Native American heritage and culture. I eventually made it to the eagle's nest, but I was a little dismayed to find the nest was just a flat 2x2 landing on the very edge of the butte. Cedar tree limbs and bones littered the area. Despite my fear, it was an amazing view. The Navajo kids were great climbers, and they just hopped around the butte like little rabbits.

SCOOPING POOP FOR JESUS

I remember a corral at Lillian and Edward's home. Fresh from the washboard express lane, the California team found the corral had not been cleaned out in years. We chopped at layers of hardened, petrified poo and the stench was still simmering under layers of trapped droppings that had been heated up at approximately 100 degrees in the middle of July. Are you picturing the scene? The kids had handkerchiefs to cover their faces, with little chance for any breaths of fresh air. The wind picked up in the afternoon, creating quite a bit of poo dust that just encapsulated our bodies. It left us smelling like a sheep pen for a few hours until we had a chance to shower.

The faithful teens continued to take out the droppings in a wheelbarrow. For those who didn't grow up on a farm, it was the first time they caught a glimpse of the scene Jesus' birth: the manger with animals and their stalls, and yes, droppings. The King of Kings was born in a setting not unlike a sheep pen!

What a humbling image. It is the text of **Philippians 2**, which says Jesus "made Himself nothing, taking the very nature of a servant, being made in human likeness, but without sin." If that were not enough, He was obedient to death—even death on a cross. Our California work team demonstrated both humility and obedience that day by cleaning the corral. I pray that the scene does not soon leave my mind, and that it may remind me to faithfully and obediently enter the sheep pens of everyday life.

GATHERING THE GIRLS AND FRYBREAD

As the day went on and the girls escaped the clutches of the sheep pen, Lillian like the good shepherd came out and gathered the girls for a time of discipleship. Lillian is in her seventies and had the girls and ladies huddle around her as she sat in her wheelchair in the heat of the day. She began to tell them her story, and encouraged them to put off the things of this world and pursue a godly man.

She told the girls how her parents made her boyfriend wait on her for three years. During that time, the young couple could see each other once a year at Christmas. Her boyfriend honored her parents' request, and they were eventually married and remain so to this day. It is almost inconceivable to wait on your future spouse with such patience. Isn't it ironic that Christ is so patient to wait for us, His Bride.

After pouring into them from the Word and her life, it was time to fill the group's stomachs. There's nothing like good ole frybread with a little powdered sugar and honey. Or, if you're from the Rez, just salt. The ladies watched as Lillian flipped the dough into little balls ready to be deep fried in lard, or shortening for a nicer term. You can just feel your arteries clog as you eat this bread like an elephant ear, but it is quite tasty and a must have for any newcomer to the Rez.

TUMBLEWEED AND A GLIMPSE OF JESUS

Sunflower Butte sits in a little valley surrounded by buttes, and by 2:30 p.m. it felt like Death Valley. The heat was boiling with no wind and the kids back at the ranch were grumbling about "slave labor" while they pulled weeds. Tumbleweed that is, thorny to touch and bearing bullheads. After they dry up, they get in your shoes and become lodged in the bottom of your feet. We walked around the corner to find Lillian out in 100 plus degree heat, telling her grandchildren how to pull weeds.

I had to stop for a moment and remind the youth pastor with me to tell his kids what we just witnessed before our eyes. Lillian was out in her corn-field being a great steward of her crops by tending to its needs. The teens were back at the mission praying they wouldn't pass out from heat exhaustion and dehydration, but later came out to Lillian's and helped pull weeds. I suppose perspective plays its part. We approached Lillian, and she slowly walked to meet us after finishing her instructions to her grandson.

Edward had recently returned home from the hospital and was not doing well. We made it to the house with Lillian, who was winded at that point. She has a tendency to become faint with over exertion. As the youth pastor, Bill Kearney and I sat with Lillian and Edward, we felt as if we were sitting at the feet of Jesus, sharing in the lives of others. I sat on the right side of Edward's bed, and Kearney sat on Lillian's left side just across from me.

Lillian expressed her concerns about her husband's health, but she also knew that her prayers had already prolonged his life. The doctors had not given Edward much time. Lillian also shared about the joy that she had in Jesus in this life. She was a living example of what it means to embrace Christ as our source of strength. I watched the way Lillian looked at the pastor, and there was a gleam in her eye like no other I had seen. I saw Jesus that day in Lillian, in her faith and in her story.

I thought of one word as we left Lillian's house that day: *faith*. Her joy was complete even as her husband's health was failing, and her testimony of faith has remained strong. Paul writes in **Galatians 5:6** that faith expressing itself in love is what really counts. Lillian's faith has been lived out so boldly over the years for His glory. According to Paul, she has found what really matters.

WATER SPRAY AND ANOTHER REZ SUNSET

On another journey out to Sunflower Butte, we held a Bible school program for the young children. Lillian was ecstatic to make a craft with the young children. She also really enjoys singing. As we sang with the children on her front door step, she reminded us of the classic kid's song, "If we all work together, together…" It was a fitting song to encourage the young Navajo children to sing His praises during our tending of the corral and cornfield.

When we were wrapping up the day's work, I went to get a drink from the water hose. Lillian was there too, and she deviously whispered "Look out, I'm gonna spray them with water." She took the hose and began blasting all who were in range with water. The group scrambled to get the thousand dollar plus camera out of the middle of the attack. She had such a joy in her heart that came out through her laughter. She worshipped God even in the sudden water sprays of life. I had to stall and take a blast of water so the camera would be safe, but it was great fun. Lillian shared her life story again as the whole team *sat at the feet of Lillian and Edward.* Another day ends at Sunflower Butte as we look back and see the dust of washboard roads and the sunset paint colors in the sky.

CALVARY'S GAZE

Our ministry with the Navajo had lasted a mere six months, and the celebration of Easter was approaching when we heard about the sunrise service. Foster children meant getting up early for school bus rides each morning, but getting up before the crack of dawn was a new experience. Heather stayed back with the kids while I forged ahead to worship God in one of my most memorable moments on the Reservation.

The weather forecast called for partly freezing and shivering, but we managed on our trek up a winding trail to a stand alone butte. The butte in my heart has been named Calvary, but I am unsure of the actual Navajo name.

Lillian had been told by her doctors not to walk too much or to do anything too strenuous because of her back. When I reached the top of the trail with my frosted lungs still adapting to the six thousand feet elevation, Lillian and others had already arrived and were building a fire to keep us warm. The glow and splendor of His glory awaited as we celebrated the Resurrection of the Light of the World.

We shared testimonies of God's greatness, and as I reflected upon the colors of the fire I noticed halfway up the butte a wooden cross. It was like sitting below Jesus' feet as he hung upon the cross, gazing up into dark blue sky with the moon still hovering over the crest of the mountainside. My heart was grateful for the privilege to sit with the Navajo in that moment.

Lillian shared that no doctor could stop her faith in God's ability to help her up the butte to worship God. Through tears, she shared her testimony and life of faith through years of trial during which she persevered in His strength. The warmth of the sun broke over the mesas to the east and began to warm our ears a bit, and we sang songs of thanksgiving in English and in Navajo. The Dine' language is so beautiful and I realized our ministry was just beginning on the Reservation.

WHERE I FIRST SAW THE LIGHT

After this Easter experience with my new Navajo family, I began to ponder what the journey might entail for our work teams if they had to walk by faith. The Word tells us to focus on the author and perfecter of our faith and on what is unseen. But what does that look like in our world today? God planted a seed to take our teams on a journey of faith to trust Him and let go of self and fear just for a moment by means of a simple blindfold.

I wish I could describe the looks we got from the local Navajos who would drive by and see bilaganas (white folk) blindfolded in a fifteen passenger van, seemingly being driven out to slaughter by my Navajo co-workers. Some pastors laughingly questioned our level of trust and exactly where we were going, but we assured them the exercise was for their spiritual growth and would be a time of worship to exalt our King.

The drive was only a few miles to an old butte with a cross and our Navajo staff would lead the team on the trail up the butte unable to see the cross and landing. Upon arrival, they remained blindfolded as we responded in worship from songs and the Word of God.

I remember one lady who was mature in years with great grey haired wisdom. She declared there was no way she would have walked up the butte if she had first seen it with her own eyes. Faith was required to follow the person ahead of you with only your right hand on their shoulder. The journey ended at the cross of Christ where we all first saw the light.

As the groups were led slowly and the group members leaned on each other for guidance, our co-workers went ahead and prepared for the reading of the Word and music to praise God. When the group reached the top, we began with singing and entered in to a time of challenge and introspection.

COMMUNION WITH GOD

It is an amazing and humbling experience to offer communion to another individual. We shared communion with each work group that participated in the "walk of faith" on the Rez. Each new group was another part of the Body of Christ, standing before the cross and reflecting on His sacrifice. They recalled Jesus' words, "Do this in remembrance of me," as they removed their blindfolds and took the bread and the cup. I saw hearts broken in that moment, with tears streaming down faces because of the wonder of the cross and the beauty of our redemption.

God really spoke to my heart through **1 Timothy 4:13-15** during one of these worship experiences on the Rez. We are commanded to devote ourselves to the public reading of Scripture, to preach and teach and to *NOT NEGLECT* our gifts. Be diligent in these matters. Verse fifteen says that if we will give ourselves wholly to Him, then everyone will see our progress and they will praise our Father in Heaven. It is for His glory that we serve and give away our lives. Whatever you do in life, do not neglect your gift. Use it for His glory.

After everyone took some time to gaze upon the cross and share communion, we headed out on the butte to spend some alone time with God in prayer and to reflect upon what had just happened in our walk with Christ. We led the groups to a time of a silence to take stock of His majesty in our lives as we looked out over grand mesas and old volcanic formations. **Zephaniah 3:17** tells us that He will quiet us in His love. The unparalleled views and the stillness on the Rez created a sense of the Father, Son and Holy Spirit working in our hearts, and His voice sounded so near.

It is amazing how God can work when your heart is broken and you surrender all you have on bended knee, letting go of every crown through tears that fall on old volcanic rocks. Our souls were refreshed **(Philemon 1:7)** and we leaned into the arms of the Lord.

Many people responded with expressions of forgiveness of others and healing in their lives as a result of letting go of the pride in their lives. They were free by trusting in Jesus sacrifice and redemption from their sins as they gazed upon the cross, we now call Calvary Butte.

GO TO THE TOP

I was with a church group from North Carolina when I sensed something in the kids. I felt God moving me to share during our devotion time out on the butte, and I told them I was praying for someone in the group who was hurting.

As I went out to pray on the butte, God spoke to my heart and revealed that I too had been given victory through His Son. I can live joyfully and abundantly, with patience and self-control, as a man of integrity that is on fire for the Lord. I thank God for showing me the difference between living on fire for Christ and just existing in my faith. As the Word tells us in **1 Thess. 5**, we should "be joyful always, pray continually and give thanks in all circumstances for it is the will of God in Christ Jesus."

After I closed in prayer on the butte that night, I felt the Lord speak to me once again as I was on my way down to the landing. As I looked to the top of the mountain I remembered a kid who had gone all the way up. It was if God was exclaiming, "Go to the top!"

The breeze was blowing stronger the higher I climbed. When the young man came into view I whistled for him to come over and I took a moment to share my testimony with him. When I was done with my story, I asked if I could pray for him. He took the opportunity to share that he was in the midst of a struggle against an addiction.

The Lord opened that young man's heart that night, and his wall of pride was toppled to make way for a peace in his heart about sharing his story. All praise to God, as He is the One who gives us the courage to let go of fear and confess our sins to our brothers in Christ. It is a freeing moment. Bonhoeffer writes in *Life Together* that confessing is "enough if shared to one brother who represents the church." My life has been blessed by accountable men, as we have broken bread and shed tears together, and we have become lost in His compassion.

CHAPTER 5

SELFISHNESS IN LIFE AND MARRIAGE

SELFISHNESS:

As the years go by, I see more clearly how selfish I can be in my marriage. A battle rages as we fight to let go of self and my wants or desires. We have to fight to put our concerns behind others, even our spouse. It seems that couples in their twenties come out of college and head into marriage without a realistic concept of compromise. At that point in my life, my being revolved around me and my schedule. Our inward focus is perpetuated by the little choices we make everyday to benefit our interest.

Little things like where to go to eat or what movie to see. This is hugely important for new relationships. I need my gadget for the video game console, but how much is the salon shampoo you want? Go to Dollar General, we're on a budget. But they don't sell X-box at the Dollar General. The battles we choose to fight sometimes...

On a more serious note, our selfishness, mostly for men and the leaders of our households, will rear its head in the amount of *time* we spend with our wife and children. My wife catches me on the third "DAD" before I snap out of my ever so important "was I productive" mode and hear my son who so desperately wants my attention.

Men and Husbands, we have to remove our selfish pride and realize that career and prestige don't love us as much as our wives and children. Our family members are the ones who really know our hearts. They know how we speak to them and how we treat them on a daily basis. How much time are you setting aside for your children who are right in front of you everyday? Sadly, even those of us who have good intentions still fall short. But we are shown grace as they forgive and love us in spite of our shortcomings.

Lord, help me to let go of self and my schedule to really hear my son and love my wife. Hold me accountable to your imitation. All the kingdoms we make on earth will pass away, so help me not to stake my treasure on what is meaningless here. May the worth of my family and my unique leadership role of husband and dad override any false promise that the world offers.

SECURITY BLANKETS AND ROOM #4

Sometimes you can't explain why an experience rocks your world as much as it does. A great friend and I went to see a potential community ministry partner today. When we arrived, my friend informed me that we were going to visit a student at the hospital who had sustained some serious injuries to his skull and brain in a skateboarding accident.

In my selfishness, my thoughts that morning had been about what seemed to be a dramatic moment in my world. I had misplaced my wallet. My son prayed about the devastating situation, and within a few minutes my wife located the missing security blanket. My son called as I was driving to my accountability group meeting and mercifully ended my self-inflicted suffering. After processing the good news, I wasn't really excited about driving downtown to meet with the prospective ministry partner without the sacred wallet in my pocket, but I didn't have much of a choice. God had some bigger things in mind for the day.

When we arrived at the hospital, we buzzed in to enter the intensive care room. As we walked in, I noticed a woman give my friend a sort of double take and she stopped to ask if he was a part of our church ministry. He told her that he was, and she teared up and shared that her aunt had been placed on life support after what was supposed to be a routine neck surgery and she needed prayer. We agreed to stop by the room, although we ended up needing a nurse ourselves when we forgot the room number.

Entering the intensive care unit is like stepping into a surreal tunnel where life and death meet. Prayer and perspective no longer seem optional. We were thankful to find James doing relatively well following his skate-boarding mishap. We prayed with him and he was able to respond.

We then made our way to Room #4. As we entered, the unresponsive woman's husband was in tears by his wife's bed, realizing that the options, and time, were limited. I immediately began to tear up, and all I could do was hold his hand. My petty wallet world came crashing down as I befriended a complete stranger in what was likely the lowest moment of his life. I began to think, where is my faith?

Husband and wife become one, and for one to be faced with the prospect of losing all you know and what you have become together in life is unfathomable. The thought of almost losing a child in an accident also went through my mind. As we walked out we pondered a question that is probably not all that unusual for those who visit the ICU. What would we do if we only had thirty days left on earth?

A great poet once wrote that we must treat the imposters of triumph and tragedy the same. This woman faced a routine surgery for her neck and she ends up in a tragic coma. Will we face tragedy with the same worship of God as in the triumph? I asked God to restore her brain waves. Would He raise her up like Lazarus, or was He drawing her husband to Him through this tragedy? In this moment words were scarce, and I walked away feeling as if I had been punched in the gut. How do you pull the plug on your better half?

God, forbid and forgive my wallet melodrama as others suffer, and may we fix our eyes on the eternal glory and hope in Christ. For our light and momentary troubles are achieving for us an eternal glory that far out-weighs them all from **2 Cor. 4:17**.

What will you do with the rest of your days?

PRIDE OF MARRIAGE

Work Overload

It seems that as the workload gets heavier, the days become shorter and the stress we bring home is overbearing. Patience is thin when dad needs space to process the work day and mom is about to fall over from taking care of the kids. Our daily routine consumes us, and we take for granted what is right in front of us.

We mean well, but as time goes on the drama builds and either spouse can begin to feel they are not getting the attention they deserve. Whether it's mom giving too much time to the kid's needs or dad pouring all his energy into his work, the other spouse feels deprived. So he brings the work home and she feels second to the prestige he wants from his career.

In this revolving door, our lives are thrown out of balance. Before we know it, our relationships suffer and marriages are on the rocks. And it all started with the small things that added up to frustration. We search for substitutes when what we really need is to focus on the real thing, as we are warned in **1 Timothy 3:5**.

I DESERVE BETTER

When marriage becomes a woe, each spouse quickly falls into self-pity. He might think his wife is too immersed in the kids, neglecting the house or lacking respect for him. Then, as soon as someone younger comes along, in the pride of pity he stumbles into her arms. Worse, he might fall into the devastating culture of pornography. Regardless of which path he takes, they all lead to self-destruction and the end of a marriage.

During our pouting and through several attempts to point out to the other spouse how they could make things better, one or both of the spouses eventually decides to open up to a co-worker, or even a member at church. It begins innocently enough. But then we lose sight of the steps we've taken, and the affair begins. The emotional attachment to another person results because "I deserve better," and "You're not meeting my needs or putting me first." There may be some truth to these accusations, but they are born out of past insecurities, self-focus and pride .

Husband and wife both need to submit first to God and His Word, and realize that love in marriage requires sacrifice. The husband needs to lead not with pride but with humility, and he must balance his work outside the home with his ministry to his family. Husbands and fathers need to be reading and sharing the Word with their families, staying centered in His truth.

Men, do not take your wife for granted. Appreciate her worth. Give yourself away with a servant's mindset, following the model of Christ's love for the church. Lead by example in your marriage and your wife will follow. You will find that you will both grow when you submit to God's Word. That is not to suggest that marriage doesn't require work. The baggage of the past for young marriages between two selfish and independent adults who are trying to become one will require honesty. We must confront our own fears and insecurities in order to free ourselves from the grip of pride.

MAN-PRIDE

My own selfishness has been illuminated over the last twelve years that my wife and I have been married. Love is not "me first," with your family scrambling for the leftovers because you are so tired and inward focused after a day at work. Our love should be like that of Christ - humble, gentle, patient, and bearing with one another, as we are reminded in **Ephesians 4:2**.

Men desire food and pleasure, in any order. Off we go to work or to otherwise save the world, and we expect our wife to raise the kids and handle every event at home. Reality for many revolves around the couch or favorite chair, what's for supper and bed time for the kids. But our family needs our support in the home. This means we help with discipline, and we lead devotions at night to guide our childrens' minds in His truth and for His glory. Know your income and expenses, and how to balance a checkbook. We are commanded to be good stewards of His money.

Just as the Church should rest secure in God's arms of comfort and encouragement, our wife needs our love. Ephesians tells us that wives are to submit to and respect their husbands, and husbands are to love their wives. This seemingly simple mandate is not so easy in practice, and we need to be reminded daily to put love into action through our words and by our deeds. A life coach recently told me that my son needs to see my affection towards my wife as well. Our sons need to learn how to treat and love his future bride, and that lesson is best taught by our example.

DISCIPLINE

The memory of how we were raised and past insecurities that are imbedded from our parents or peers will ultimately affect our choices in life, as well as the way we respond to our spouse and children. I am reminded of **Proverbs 13:24** that states that whoever spares the rod hates the son, but he who loves him is diligent or careful to discipline him. We must be careful and patient in our discipline and let our kids know we love them in spite of it. Actually, I recommend a wooden paddle with drilled holes for greater efficiency and aerodynamics. My dad made his own and I turned out…well, nevermind. The real key is in letting your yes be yes, and your no be no with your kids. The wisdom in this was so evident during our time with the Navajo foster children. They needed some routine and the love of discipline to guide them in their choices.

God disciplines us when we misbehave, and yet He loves us greatly. **Hebrews** chapter twelve explains that His discipline is born out of love and a desire that we would someday share in His holiness. Discipline is painful, but it does eventually produce a harvest of righteousness and peace.

NAVAJO TACOS AND A BUMPY REZ RIDE

Foster care continued even as Heather neared full term in her pregnancy. We had - count them - five kids in the children's home. We survived that summer of endless sixteen plus hour days only by His grace. It was an exciting time as the due date approached, and our parents flew out to see us. But the due date came and went, and it looked like they would have to return home before the baby arrived. Thank God for the Navajo Taco that Heather ate one evening. It probably brought on the contractions later that night just before midnight. I remember the night vividly as Heather woke up and declared, "I am having contractions." Of course, I had to say something intelligent in the moment, so I asked "Are they less than 5 minutes apart?" Needless to say, Heather was soon struggling to get into the vehicle for the hour plus drive to the mission hospital in Ganado. I woke up her parents as mine were headed to the Grand Canyon, not aware that the baby would arrive that night, and we were soon out on the open range of the Rez.

We got to the hospital and of course Dad (that's me now) had the camcorder in Heather's face as she could barely get out of the car. She has never seen the value of the footage, ready-made for YouTube (lucky for her, that had not been established yet). The contractions lasted from 11:30 p.m. until the next evening at 6:00 p.m. when she finally began pushing for another hour! The baby did crown with a full head of black hair, but not enough horsepower. This kid was not coming out. So they gave Heather a drug to increase her contractions, only to then wait some more. Finally, the decision was made to perform an emergency C-section - 60 MILES AWAY!

Her contractions were increasing like a lightning storm in the body, and physically Heather was worn out. I had to raise my voice for her to push during the first delivery attempt just to keep her from falling asleep from physical exhaustion. It was near midnight when we began our ambulance ride to Rehobeth Christian Hospital in an Gallup, New Mexico, of course on a beat up and broken road.

When we arrived at 1:00 a.m. an emergency C-section team was brought in. I remember a nurse coming over to me right before Heather went into the operating room, and she asked if she could pray with me. I was so relieved and felt His comfort as she prayed for the surgery and the birth of our child. We went into the OR, and I sat by Heather's right side. Thankfully the curtain was up at her mid-section.

I opted not to watch as they retrieved our child. The doctor asked, "Do you know the sex?" We told him we did not, and He said the most beautiful words exclaimed through this whole ordeal: "It's a boy!" I thought we were having a girl, which would have been fine, but my prayer was for a little man and we got just that, Elias Mason Stewart. Our little Rez boy was given the Navajo name Ashkii Chezintlah, which means "Little boy in the midst of the mountains."

Haven't our lives been like that beat up and broken road? Sure, there have been some smooth spots. But there have also been some bumps along the way. Sometimes all we can do is hold on to Christ during the storm, and, like Job, worship Him no matter what trial or petty problem has exploded in our small world. We come together as the Bride of Christ to form this broken road that leads us on the pathway to God, each doing his part as the perfect Father uses his imperfect children to further His Kingdom. That is just one aspect of the amazing grace and unfathomable love that we received in the gift of His Son.

The wall of pride crumbles a little more even in the birth of a child. The event helps us see creation through God's eyes, and we are able to better understand our reliance on our Creator as He holds our lives and the universe in balance.

CHAPTER 6:

JEALOUSY, ENVY AND WOE'S INSECURITY

COMPETING GREEN-EYED MONSTER DRAGONS

Anger is cruel and fury overwhelming, but who can stand before jealousy.—Proverbs 27:4

Moreover, accusations like the woman's always seem to spring from the <u>jealousies that great scarcity inspires.</u> The accused son lives in a better ti kay than his mother. In effect, she was saying this son didn't care about his mother, so he must have been the one who sent sorcery to kill his brother.

These kinds of allegations, accusations that arise out of economic inequalities, are common, Farmer says. They can tear families and friends apart. **Mountains beyond Mountains,** Kidder

I believe that in impoverished areas such as the Rez, the affluence of one person or family creates intense jealousies that can and have led to false accusations. During our experience on the Navajo Reservation, we saw individuals accused of molestation by close family members. That is an accusation which obviously devastates all appearance of integrity and promotes distrust of that person throughout the community as well as with the family.

Our work team case studies on pride always boiled down to three major categories which we will discuss a little later. Jealousy and envy was the second largest category noted. We had participants write out their true torments and inhibitions which led them to assert that the green-eyed monster of jealousy continues to be a struggle.

What leads to jealousy in the greatest arenas of your life? Besides the whole drama of your significant other - stay tuned, we'll come back to that genre. Where are you most days all day if not in school? Probably at work. The effort of your life, where you put your energy and dreams. How do you think pride begins to rear its head in the 'office'?

JUICES OF COMPARISON AND COMPETITION

A new officer is hired at the bank, or a new staff member joins your team. Perhaps they just finished their MBA. You feel threatened, or maybe fear sets in, and you suddenly feel a need to prove your worth and talent.

It's amazing how pride forms. It goes back to our childhood days of playing baseball or basketball, while our dads yelled at us to do better and try harder. Competition is forced down our throats whether we like it or not. This is just the American way. Pride is the fuel that drives the competitive spirit within us.

Competition can be healthy. We can channel our competitive spirit to compete at the Olympic level, striving to be the best in the world at some individual event. But that's not the type of competition we're talking about. Our focus here is the competition that is harmful. If your competitive spirit follows the path from envy to jealousy to self-destruction, then it is probably not healthy.

Think of the term "eval," a word that is dreaded in the business world. No one wants to deal with the yearly evaluation, and yet they exist. We put up with them for the reward - the raise at year end. The corporation loves it because they believe that comparison among co-workers will drive employees to work harder. The hope is that competition in the workplace will improve productivity.

This is where personality traits are really important. Maybe for you, this eval and competition truly revs your engine and inspires you to excel and perform at a greater level.

But for some, that same competition can lead to envy that burns to jealousy, and the results are strife and fear of replacement. Then, the old "lack of recognition" kicks in as we compare our worth to that of others. The road leads to self-pity - woe is me. Brennan Manning describes this progression from self-pity to self-hatred in *Ruthless Trust* better than any other author I've read to date:

"The more guilt and shame that we have buried within ourselves, the more compelled we feel to seek relief through sin. As we fixate on our jaded motives and soiled conscience, our self-esteem sinks, and in a pernicious leap of logic, we think that we are finally learning humility.

On the contrary, a poor self-image reveals a lack of humility. Feelings of insecurity, inadequacy, inferiority, and self-hatred rivet our attention on ourselves. Humble men and women do not have a low opinion of themselves; they have no opinion of themselves, because they so rarely think of themselves."

As we went through the pride studies with our work groups on the Reservation, my eyes were opened to this amazing truth that our "woe is me" is really a focus on self, and thus pride. It's like we drown in the sea of woe, tossed about because our attention is not on God, but on us. 'I' seems to be our primary concern, and Manning is right.

We cling to whatever pleases us in an effort to stay afloat in that sea of woe. We cover the pain or self-hatred with instant gratification and satisfaction. We want to look like we have it all together. But letting go of self and humbly walking with God in fear of Him, living for His glory and not our image, will allow for that radical self-acceptance that we desire. Humility is not having a low opinion of self, but rather having NO opinion of self as we look to the author and perfecter of our faith.

He truly loves us as we are, whether someone else deems us a 1 or a 5 on the 'eval' scale. May we let go of the pride necklace, whether it is all is me or woe is me. Otherwise, we will sink in the sea of self, destined to never really live in the freedom that has been provided by Christ by the forgiveness of our sins. Look to the strengths God has given you. Humbly live for His glory, not what this world sells through sex appeal and more stuff. Let Him be your sufficient God of comfort. Find peace in a *radical love affair* with Jesus, who will never leave you nor forsake you.

As the Body of Christ, we should model this relationship and life of love. As Paul writes in Galatians, "the only thing that counts is faith expressing itself through love" (**Gal. 5:6**).

GUITAR HEROES AND DANGEROUS CHORDS

I remember watching some guys on one of our work teams as they played the guitar. God had really swayed my heart with a desire to learn this six string bewilderment. A church in Indianapolis sent me a check for $150, so off to the music shop I went to buy the "beginner" guitar, complete with picks, strap and case.

I began strumming at the same time with another missionary on the field, but neither of us were feeling the vibe. After weeks of futile attempts we realized that we had to get this down before the upcoming summer so we could lead worship with our work teams. I wondered, "How is that going to happen with three chords and a prayer?" But God is so faithful, and one night we sat in my living room and practiced the first song we ever learned to play together.

WHEN THE MUSIC FADES

The song we learned that night was *The Heart of Worship* by Matt Redman. A D chord and an A, along with some rhythm. We finally learned the chord changes and how to move our fingers while actually keeping a beat. We had finally learned to play our first song. Then, previously unknown thoughts of comparison and competition came our way.

I remember us playing *Sanctuary* and *All in All* at Indian Wells for our bus ministry outreach. We were learning new songs, and with them new chords, each week. As time progressed we both began to notice that the other person was learning and playing new songs that were outside our master list. We both thought, "He knows that song, so I'll play something else that I enjoy for our worship set."

Drama ensued as the summer began and we constantly questioned whose turn it was to lead worship for a certain church team. If the group was from one of my supporting churches, then I would play despite the fact that I played the previous week. We were so blind to pride that we didn't realize it until it was too late. I had written and sung songs in our worship time with the Navajo youth and not much was said about the music. It was as if an unpublished competition was underway to see which of us

71

would make it on the top ten Reservation chart.

Another sad product of our pride occurred when I was the first one to play the electric guitar for a worship set. As excited as I was, we didn't have the sound system running well that night. We were not there for each other, and the outcome was not good for anyone in the room. I thought I had become Hendrix or something with four dangerous chords.

Do you see the great irony of pride in this story? It happens in both corporate and church leadership teams, from teaching to worship. CS Lewis writes that "it's the comparison of being better than someone else that leads to the competition," whether or not either one of you has eyes to recognize pride in the situation.

Even more ironic, the very first song we ever learned to play together was *The Heart of Worship*. Remember the words from the chorus of that song, and compare them to what we made of worship.

> I'm coming back to the heart of worship,
> And it's all about you, its all about you Jesus.
> I'm sorry Lord for the thing I made it,
> When it's all about you, its all about you Jesus.

When the music fades, as the song opens, and all is said and done on this earth, the comparison of our wealth, possessions, looks or talent will not matter. What will matter is how we loved God and our neighbor.

God forgive me for what I made it. Thank you for bringing me back to the heart of worship. May those in the wake of the dangerous chords back on the Rez find forgiveness as we strum on for the Kingdom for Jesus' glory.

THE RECREATION CENTER

SNOW FILLED FOOTERS

I remember the adventure of God helping us frail men build a youth recreation center starting in the bitter cold of February. A backhoe never looked as beautiful after prior work teams had dug the last footers by hand. Snowflakes were falling as we worked on the foundation and prepared to plant His Word through the use of a gym.

CONCRETE CRACKS AND COLLEGE STUDENTS

We were in a panic trying to form the foundation when a college age work-team from North Carolina rolled into Dilkon in mid-March. The madness of March began with concrete trucks coming down the dirt road, and stress was ordered up for the main dish. The college kids were breaking their backs. Their job entailed putting on boots and stepping in the wet sludge to level the concrete before it dried out in the windy, sun-soaked day.

The first pour from the trucks came so fast and furious that we almost lost the ability to keep it wet enough to manipulate the finish of the surface. Day two brought a scare as we poured the west corner and the wooden forms blew out. We had to halt the mud flow and immediately repair the form in order to have a square corner on the west end.

True colors came out as stress sent out flaming arrows of commands to move and stop the flow of the mud. Perhaps this is the best example of righteous anger I can think of as the facilitator had to call the troops to take action. Thankfully, the gym is still standing today, proof that God is faithful to hear the cry of His saints all these years after the Israelites labored in the mud to make bricks for Egypt.

SCISSOR LIFTS AND GUSTY APRIL DAYS OF SWAY

Once the foundation was finished, the time had come to sort out the brown steel beams that had been dropped in the field next to the slab. I praise God for the efforts and research of our facilitator who built homes for years in Illinois. But he had never taken on the endeavor of a 16,000 square foot steel and metal building. You know the old saying, "April showers bring May flowers." Well, April on the Rez brings WIND, period. Almost every day in April and May, wind gusts range from twenty to thirty miles an hour with dust blowing and entering structures even through locked windows.

The tinker toy fun began with following instructions that told us to raise two 25-foot beams in the air with a cross-cable brace. We performed this feat with God, a crane operator, our facilitator, and two Navajo men. We tied cables to a parked bus to anchor the first two beams. Total Rez dog style and OSHA approved I'm sure. We never had tie offs even though we worked thirty feet up in the air and a local Navajo man walked the beams. Crazy times. It all would have fallen over if not for God's grace.

April days got exciting as we fought the increasingly strong winds. We worked from 5 a.m. until 6 p.m. for seven days one week. The winds would be calm early, but then the gusts began to increase. I had never heard of a scissor lift, but it is a hydraulic machine that fittingly scissor lifts up to thirty-five feet. As the day wore on we found ourselves stuffing bolts up in the air, swaying from the gusts and hoping the scissor lift would not tumble over. My body's vertigo was still moving when I returned to shower at night.

The seventh day in a row was Sunday and no one wanted to work that day. We set out, but one of the men said it was just too much. The mornings were cold and windy, and our bodies were shot from the elements and the swaying. But we were determined to persevere for the sake of Christ. After prayer and supplication, we pressed on that day. Our task was to connect the west end so the recreation center could be wood framed on the inside by a team from Georgia.

Every task worth fighting for to further the Kingdom will require some sacrifice or hard work. To date, our lives have yet to experience the sacrificial cup of Christ.

SOLID ROCK'S ALICE COOPER AND REZ BASKETBALL

Eventually, the side walls were up. Although we lacked a roof, we held our first ever Spark Youth Night in May with a team from Las Vegas. Oh the joy of water balloon fights and football in the gym. Football because the basketball goals had yet to arrive for installation. The gym also had dorm rooms for our work teams with laundry facilities, a nice kitchen, aerobic and weight room, game room and computer lab.

The Body of Christ continued to give and provide help all summer. In the fall we were able to snap in a hard plastic vinyl floor for the basketball court. The ministry was fully operational, and many youth who normally would not hear of the grace and truth of Christ at church started to find His love on the Navajo Reservation inside a recreation center.

Spring of 2005 came, and the time of our celebration and of blessing the gym's inception came from the Solid Rock Foundation. That Foundation alone donated over $150,000 to the project. The Navajo Christian Foundation was excited as we prepared to host Alice Cooper and his board members with Solid Rock. They arrived on a big bus and we unloaded their belongings, as reporters from regional newspapers arrived to interview James, our director, and Alice Cooper.

We opened the day with a basketball game between NCF's staff and Solid Rock. Alice had the Navajo children come out of the stands and shoot free throws. The day was a blessing as that night Alice performed some of his hits from over the years and sang for the first time in public with his son's band.

James had me present to Alice a Navajo rug which had Solid Rock Foundation woven into the design as a much appreciated thank you for their fundraising efforts that enabled us to complete the recreation center. More than five hundred people showed up that day, and I remember walking out with Alice after the concert and him noting the beauty and brightness of the moon. I thanked him for his efforts and willingness to help our mission and he signed a Route 66 metal emblem for me.

The light of that full moon still shines down on Dilkon today, and on the gym that reflects the True Light of Christ for the Navajo Nation.

YOUTH LEADERS BEWARE!!

One thing that is not being taught to students absorbed in the world of peer pressure and conformity to cool is the end result of not meeting those expectations. The insecurities (woes) that are formed when we feel like we don't measure up come out of the mocking and disapproval of our peers. Strengths are formed when we feel the acceptance of those same peers. Teachers, sport coaches and parents pour their character into students, but kids continue to find their worth in affirmation from their peers.

CUT TO FEEL

Take yourself back to high school for a moment. We competed for every-thing. This is the structure of our world, from art, dance, sports, girlfriend or boyfriend. We fought for attention and affirmation, yearning for "cool," seeking to fit into a crowd. The real danger is for the kids who find no common ground or feel they don't meet the requirements.

Think of the cheerleader who doesn't quite stay under the 100 pound club. Add to that the false love drama with her boyfriend. What is such a girl to do in our culture? Too often, she turns to cutting herself to express the pain and heartache inside. I remember sitting with her on our stage as she pulled up her sleeves to show me her arms.

We may be missing the point in our discipleship of students. We bring the lights and the programs and perhaps even good Biblical teaching, but we are always "talking" as leaders. When was the last time you scheduled some of your time with a kid and really *listened to this student*? These kids are hurting the same way you and I were back in the day. The drama has not changed for their lives – it has only gotten worse, with more tech-nology and higher expectations coming from all angles.

My Navajo students on the Reservation were polled and asked what brought their spirits down. The overwhelming response from the students fell into three categories: family, friends and school. Of all things, our own family drama is bringing down the ones we are trying to raise up. Our culture has put the fun in dysfunction, creating a whirlwind in student's hearts. *Then they feel and believe they are to blame or they blame God, and you can then see why it's so hard for them to know if God is real in their lives.*

Many kids are hurt by parents who out of selfishness do not take the time to listen. Lack of encouragement leads to discouragement for children, and is a direct result of the sin of selfishness and pride. Pain, anger, and disappointment can lead children to make bad conscious choices. In my own life, after my parents split when I was in high school, I didn't cut my wrists to numb the pain because alcohol felt better at the time.

SELF PITY TO HATRED AND DESTRUCTION

But it gets worse. What led to the tragedy at Columbine? Those kids were hurting bad, but they were not finding community and love like we find in Christ. But was anyone listening to those young men? Following the progression described by Brennan Manning, their pain and woe moved from insecurity to self-pity, on to self-hatred and then to some form of self-destruction. In their case, the self-destruction phase took the form of pulling a trigger.

Wake up, Church. This is not a worship buzz from good music or bigger pizza parties or "cool' youth events. It will take removing the veil even from the leadership to be transparent if we are going to reach the next generation. Then it will mean *LISTENING!* The opportunity to write down what is in their heart, or to sit with a group leader who will *make the time* to listen is a good start. At least create an opportunity for youth to respond in a safe place so they can be encouraged and comforted by the Word.

Most students, and people in general, respond to life out of emotion. As we find grace and love in the midst of all the junk, we can begin to move past ourselves and look up to find the open arms of Christ and His acceptance. But it starts with listening to each other, and truly caring when the person across from us is sharing their story.

> *The heart of humility lies in undivided attention to God, a fascination with his beauty revealed in creation, a contemplative presence to each person who speaks to us, and a "de-selfing" of our plans, projects, ambitions, and soul.* ***(Ruthless Trust)***

The formula only works when we take ourselves out of the picture, and respond to others with an attention and affection that flows out of our worship of God. We must put God and His Kingdom first, and then take what He gives and pour into those around us.

PRESENT DARKNESS AND THE TRUE LIGHT

As I have walked with the Navajo there have been moments of oppression and attacks that I have not been able to face alone. With one summer work group we decided to have a one day fast in prayerful remembrance of what our Navajo youth were facing in their lives. One team member on a first time visit penned these words about his experience on the Rez:

> *One evening after all the kids had left (from the gym), I went outside to enjoy what was left of the evening sky. I looked west and saw a long, black cloud hanging over the buttes and mesas along the horizon. Black, finger-like sections of this cloud were reaching down toward the land. At first I was impressed with this uniquely western silhouette, but it suddenly reminded me of the cover of Frank Peretti's novel, **This Present Darkness**.*
>
> *I thought about how Satan is after these people, too, and seeks to keep them in darkness any way he can. I thought about the government sponsored massacres and murders, oppression and treaty-breaking, theft of the best native lands, and ongoing prejudices against these people. I said aloud, 'Lord, I wish we (meaning white people) had never come here and hurt them. But almost immediately God reminded me that through white people and natives, He has been sending them His love and the Gospel of Jesus Christ for many years.'*

I'm reminded of **John 8** where Jesus describes the devil as a murderer from the beginning, not holding to the truth, for there is no truth in him. When he lies, he speaks his native language, for he is a liar and the father of lies, He tells us in verse **forty-four**. He creeps and sneaks into the lives of all of us through media, television and the internet and we begin to believe the lies that we must have wealth and beauty to enjoy life.

The woe that the enemy tries to instill in the hearts and minds of our youth is devastating to the point of self-destruction, and so many are lonely and crying out for attention. They crave unconditional love. They buy the lie that they are not loved, that they are unwanted or ugly in the sight of the world. Yet our Savior ransomed his life out of love for His children.

Those of us who know this truth can't help but *shine the true light* (see **1 John 2:8**).

Further, we read that "Anyone who claims to be in the light but hates his brother is still in the darkness. Whoever loves his brother lives in the light, and there is nothing in him to make him stumble." The true light is already shining, and it should be reflected in our lives as we spend time with those who are crushed in spirit and brokenhearted.

IMAGINARY DISTRESSES: MORE STEAK FROM LEWIS

In the darkness of their woe and self-pity, teens and young adults are feeling low. As expressed by one college student's feedback from our pride study, "I had people all around me and yet felt so lonely, depressed and just ready to take my own life." Although sometimes they will put on a mask to try to hide their pain, we need to be mindful to ask the hard questions, to slow down and really get to know their story.

Sometimes, as CS Lewis writes, there are 'imaginary distresses' that come up in the midst of self-pity. I recently read this in the *Screwtape Letters,* and I had to put the book down to reflect on this profound thought. We so often overcomplicate events that have yet to occur, and in our mind these imaginary distresses weigh us down and keep us second-guessing out of fear. Questions come up like, "Should I say this?" or "Is my cool on?"

If you have walked down this path or swam in this sea yourself, you know how true this is. Maybe you have known others who deal with this distress every day, imagining the divorce that is coming or the dreaded break-up which surely means they are neither loved nor beautiful. The distresses become so magnified in our minds. I vividly remember as a teenager being told about my parents' divorce. The news came from my dad in our living room, and it went on to wreck my high school years. Yes, these are actual events in our lives, but in the woe of self-pity and the icing on the cake of insecurity, we envision imaginary distresses and give these trials a measure of power over us that they were never meant to have.
Another student from the Rez pride study told their story this way:

"My devastation and self-pity took control of my heart, attitude, actions, and life. I was so consumed by the anger I felt towards the rest of the world for continuing to move, grow, and find the love of God while my whole world continued to fail."

The imaginary distresses CS Lewis mentioned can move out of self-pity to self-hatred from a lack of contentment proving the move to self-destruction.

HAVASUPAI AND EMERALD GREEN SWIMMING POOLS

Every year our interns would go on a wild western adventure, not really knowing all the details before heading out. Our cowboys caught a ride with a church group to Flagstaff and then off we went past Seligman to Supai point. The goal was about a ten mile hike to Havasu falls and then another two miles to Mooney Falls.

The Falls are located on the Havasupai Indian Reservation at the bottom of the Grand Canyon. Stop and think for a moment about living in a canyon surrounded by walls over six hundred feet high. The people who live there are dependent on a helicopter that delivers goods to the village. The helicopter is the most efficient way to receive products; otherwise they hike or ride horseback to Supai point.

We began our hike around sunset, near 7:45 p.m., and hiked for almost two hours before finding a place to slept along the trail. A fellow cowboy got bit by some critter but he survived, and we all laid on our backs and talked as we watched the stars. Over about two hours we saw seven shooting stars. We were amazed by God's fingerprints across the sky. His Word tells us in **Psalm 147:4** that "He determines the number of the stars and calls them each by name."

The next morning, like a shot of java in the veins, we were up at 4:45 a.m., ready to finish the march to the Havasupai. It was so early that we entered their reservation at 6:30 a.m. and no one was working the counter to accept the twenty spot for the entry fee. Our eyes fell upon Havasu falls, with its images of pristine emerald green-blue water. I must add that no one else was there at seven in the morning!

God was saying to us, "Ahhhhh….here are some precious pools my young brothers, swim, immerse yourselves in my creation." We had the whole place to ourselves for an hour and we felt like the old frontiersman Powell. We swam behind the waterfall in really rough waters, holding on to the side for help. Behind the falls, I climbed onto a slippery moss covered rock and dove into the water where the fall broke on the water's surface.

The beautiful natural coves of limestone, which create the color of the water, looked like something you would see in the garden of Eden. "A river watering the garden flowed from Eden; from there it was separated into four headwaters," just as described in Genesis 2:10. In one area, the water fell over a limestone edge into a circular limestone bed about four feet deep. The force of the water was strong enough to create a natural whirlpool, providing a nice massage after our calves had locked up from the ten mile hike.

MOONEY FALLS AND DEHYDRATING DILEMMAS

After some time enjoying Havasu, we scurried off to Mooney Falls which has its own distinct look with brown, volcanic lava dripping rock face. We had to hold on to a chain staked into the rock wall with small indentations for footholds to get down to the bottom of the canyon. The falls drop around two hundred feet and the force of the water was intense as we swam out to the center. It felt like we were caught in a storm out at sea.

It was comforting to know we were not in any real danger, unlike being in the middle of the ocean, because we had an edge to swim to. But the rush of the water near the crashing point was powerful and we had fun swimming behind the falls and enjoying God's creation.

We then made what may have been the worst decision of our young lives as we chose to hike out at 1:30 p.m. Not a good idea! I bought my last cold drink, a thirty-two ounce Gatorade, and I felt like I was tasting a piece of heaven, milking every ounce and piece of ice from my styrofoam cup. The hike was over four hours in the most brutal heat stroke prone weather imaginable – it was the middle of July in the Arizona desert. My orange delight filled with necessary electrolytes was gone in an hour. I only had some lukewarm water left for the next three hours. We wanted out of the desert so much that we only took three breaks, each around ten to fifteen minutes. When we reached the end of the trail, we stared up at the last leg of our journey – a switchback trail a thousand feet high. We suddenly felt a yearning for potassium.

For most of us, our legs were shot. One was near dehydration and beginning to cramp. None of us had cold water for this last mile. I was able to walk, but I was almost out of my lukewarm water. Near the top of the switchback I found a gallon jug that was three quarters full of HOT water. Someone had left it sitting along the trail. The water was too hot to drink, but I poured it on my head for some relief before continuing the climb to the top.

One of our guys took a two hour nap, so he ran up the switchback and watched us creep our way up. It probably helped that he was a cross-country runner, but we had played hard and swam all day.

We were all dead tired, and one person got pretty sick with sore muscles, but we all made it to the top of the trail. We were crying out to other people who were just about to start down the trail for some cold water to buy! No one had any cold water that they were willing to sell us. The drive from Supai point to the nearest cold drink was about forty-five minutes. We were cruising in our rental at like… well, way too fast.

We looked like walking stiffs, barely unable to bend our knees, by the time we entered a convenience store for refreshments. Surprisingly, the track star got sick in Flagstaff, two of us managed to hold ourselves together, and the fourth felt ill and had to get a banana to eat. We ordered some pizza and pasta for some carbs and felt human again after the intake of some food.

Havasu and Mooney Falls are truly two highlights of the great wonders found in the Grand Canyon. I recommend the trip, and I even returned despite my first adventure there, but the next time was in the cool of the evening.

A LITTLE FURTHER TO THE COLORADO RIVER

On a separate journey past Mooney Falls in the summer of 2003, we had just worked six weeks in a row with different work groups, averaging sixteen hour days. The last day we worked from 8 a.m. to 9 p.m. with a four hour drive to the "point." The next morning we embarked on a twenty-mile hike one way to the Colorado River.

Our bedtime the previous night was around 2 a.m., but that didn't stop us from leaving at on quite an adventure at 7 a.m. the next morning. Once again, we were not fully prepared for the coming experience. We make it to the rope swing past Mooney Falls when the plot began to thicken. We left dirt trails, crossed water near waist high into a sea of tall grass as thick as molasses, whisking our legs as we walked through this narrow path. Little did we realize at the time that we had missed our way on the trail.

Around 4:30 p.m., a storm began to brew. We were in the middle of the summer monsoon season. We took what appeared to be a route out of the grassy knoll. At that point, we lost all signs of a visible trail.

From a cliff edge around forty feet high, a small fall led down to where we stood next to pools of water. We were lost. Our next marker was a rope ladder, and that was enough to lead us into dismay over our location.

Suddenly, a man I'll call Billy realized he had lost his shoe. Great timing, as we were lost on a trail in the middle of nowhere watching dark clouds form above us. Claps of thunder were not far off. Billy did not want to get his hiking shoes wet in the water we would soon cross, so off he back-tracks to find his jewel of a wet sandal. It began to rain, and I sat as we prayed for the provision of Billy's sandal and relief from the weather. Would I trust God through our dilemma?

Billy heard a group across the river. The trail was above us on the other side of the rock wall, and they were heading down towards our side. The sandal is on and we were off again, headed to Beaver Falls. A young couple approached us on the trail and remarked that we were traveling light. They asked if we had any iodine tablets. Our faces must have answered the question. They helpfully explained that the tablets would purify our water from Havasu Creek.

The gracious couple provided some iodine and we continued on towards the Colorado. We were about fifteen to sixteen miles into our trek at this point with four more to go, and we were desperate to see the River. The trail ended when we reached Havasu Creek, and other mountaineers had stacked rocks to show us where our feet should step on the other side of the water.

By this time we were completely exhausted. I decided to change my shoes so my feet could be dry again. My dry feet gave me a burst of confidence and energy to press on toward the goal. The end was near as my watch ticked past 6 p.m. and we walked through a narrow tunnel onto a log with notched steps. Where is the Colorado though? Had we not walked the last four miles??

ALL MEN DIE, FEW TRULY LIVE

Perseverance led us to the end of the creek, where it narrows into a slot canyon. Finally the Colorado River was in front of us! I immediately turned to Billy and said, "Let's get in, man!" But Billy said no way. The river was raging way too fast for him, but I found an opportunity around the right side of the bank near the creek. I jumped in and persuade Billy to follow since there was no swift current in the cove where the creek flows into the rapids.

Swimming down the creek back toward the entrance of the narrow canyon, we found a thirty foot jump, but the water was not deep. I swam down about eight feet to the bottom and figured we could jump without hitting bottom. I jumped without incident and shouted to Billy, "All men die and few truly live." Wild at heart, with pride pushing us off, we jumped that day into the wilderness and mystery of God. We experienced the fullness of life and adventure, in a reckless love affair with Christ. Immersed in His unfailing love in Havasu creek, we swam to the end near the raging river.

The water from the Colorado was freezing and I slipped off the bank while I was trying to climb out, but I was able to regain a hold and made it out with just a few racked nerves. The day came to a close – we had journeyed to the Colorado River in one day and we were shot down dead tired. Our attempts at making a small fire were to no avail as our lighters were wet from crossing the creek. The choice of rocks to make our beds was not wise. We settled on top of 105 degree rocks that baked our insides as we attempted half-hour increments of sleep. The ants could have carried us off as tired as we were, but instead they took over our backpacks, devouring our peanut butter and jelly sandwiches.

ERIC AND THE JOURNEY HOME

The next day we made it back to Mooney Falls in good fashion and rested for a few hours. We had met a man named Eric on the way to Havasu, and by God's grace we found him eating alone at a café after leaving Mooney. Oh, the glory of God and His creation of cows that give us double cheese-burgers. My tasty Supai burger was over-the-top taste bud delight after thirty-six hours of grueling calf twisting trauma. It was worth much more than the $5.75 that I paid for it and some cold water.

Jeff, the local cook, ate with us and then prayed for our journey. Eric joined our table as well. He was unsure of Jesus, but said he believed in God. Billy became Graham, and we had him cornered for the plunge. We shared how Christ came to die for us even while we were still sinners. We told Eric about the people with whom Jesus held company in his day, and that by the grace of God our ransom was paid by His Son. Eric said he needed to get started up the trail, but Billy and I were grateful for planting seeds that God would later grow in his life.

The time was 5:40 p.m., day two, and our incentive to keep going was a great night's sleep in Flagstaff. We actually caught up with Eric at around 7:45 that evening at the end of the trail. Praise God, we were still alive after hiking thirty-nine miles in two days now with the switchbacks that stared us in the face. God's Word tells us to make the most of every opportunity, so we asked Eric if we could pray with him. He told us he was encouraged by our conversation with him, and I prayed that he would one day come to know the way and truth of Jesus' life unto salvation.

We said goodbye that day to the Grand Canyon and our Colorado River journey, where we experienced life as few truly live. We joined in worship of the One who gave His life without utterance or complaint. Jesus, the King of Kings and the stallion crucified, has revealed a great love to His creation.

OVERCOMING PERFORMANCE BY LIVING HIS GRACE

BONFIRES BURN THE CHAFF:

It's amazing how God moves in our hearts when we share our stories in community. One night, we assembled a teen house church group around a fall bonfire. We heard a teenage girl's story of being hurt at a young age and losing part of herself to a young man. The pain was so real in her eyes. Several of our young men also shared about their struggles with lust, and it was a great moment of God moving in the hearts of the Body.

In a previous session with our youth group, one girl mentioned how competition can arouse thoughts of "Why not me?" "The coach didn't choose me to play over 'that girl.'" "I am so much better than her." Anger turns to jealousy, and we dive into the "I don't deserve this" refrain.

We need to slow down and find ourselves in our own story. Be grateful and glad for others' successes and blessings from God. Accepting what God has given you, and use your own talents for His glory. The more we let go of our self absorption, the more open we will become to seeing others' gifts as one more part of the Body. We stop competing and no longer compare ourselves to one another, and we let go of constantly having to appear good enough. It makes you wonder why we dress up for church.

> "The longer you spend in the presence of Jesus, the more accustomed you grow to His face, the less adulation you will need because you will have discovered for yourself that He is Enough. And in the presence, you will delight in the discovery of what it means to live by grace and not by performance." (Rabbi's Heartbeat)

Read that again. **He is Enough**. We can let our pride guard down and submit to God as His people. But we must make time for prayer, solitude and fasting and find Him in the presence. As we invest in this time and find His grace, we realize that our worth comes from His unfailing love as a beloved child. (The power of grace exists and moves into our lives despite our discipline). Knowing we have something we do not deserve, we let go of living by performance and stop competing with others. One Rez team member summed it up like this: "**I was competing for glory with God**."

Men living by God's Word and leading their households begin to model a humble submission to God in the Word, at church and in how we live our lives. Families will be more inclined to follow their leadership knowing that they are exalting Him above all other creatures in worship. A right understanding of humility moves us to live for something greater than self.

> Humility is manifested in an indifference to our intellectual, emotional, and physical well-being and a carefree disregard of the image we present. No longer concerned with appearing to be good, we can move freely in the mystery of who we really are, aware of the sovereignty of God and of our absolute insufficiency and yet moved by a spirit of radical self-acceptance without self-concern.' (Ruthless Trust)

The solution to the sin of pride is to really LET GO OF SELF. Stop worrying about image and approval from the world, and move in a freedom that individually accepts you for who you are. The sovereignty of God and His Word alone is our foundation, and with Him as our refuge we rest in His grace, acknowledging the Father, absorbed in the arms of Jesus and accepting the mirror's image to reflect His glory.

Let us remember how small we are as His creatures as we worship Him, whether under a sunset sky, by a little painted desert, or looking out an airplane window. Let Him carry you through His handiwork in the clouds. Or perhaps as you sit on the side of a butte in Arizona, gazing upon the cross, humbled by the scene of Calvary. Wherever it is, may you come to know that in the presence of Jesus, you are less and He is all you need for life. May you find the mystery of grace.

CHAPTER 7:

| FEAR

FEAR and THE IMPOSTER'S MASK

Well, here I sit in the plethora of American culture, consumed by the simple desire of coffee…Starbucks. As though they need any more word of mouth advertising.

I think it's something to do with how we feel psychologically when we actually pay more than a normal price for a cup of coffee. Expense to perceived value to satisfaction to "cool." And the brewing simmers on.

I have realized through this study that we often operate not out of our strengths like we should, but from our weaknesses. The last pride category from our Rez study is *FEAR*. Fear dominates our thinking in direct proportion to the decisions we make in life. Think about it for a moment. When was the last time you made a decision to act out of a reckless courage through faith in something larger than self, not worried about what others think or how you will be *perceived* in your general pocket of influence?

We end up trying so hard to please others and gauge our day's success by others' praise or criticism. We become an imposter that wears whatever mask will suffice in the moment.

> 'Living out of the false self creates a compulsive desire to present a perfect image to the public so that everybody will admire us and nobody will know us. I have sinned in my cowardly refusal-out of fear of rejection-to think, feel, act, respond, and live from my authentic self. We even refuse to be our true self with God—and then wonder why we lack intimacy with Him. Hatred of the imposter and I constitute one person. Contempt for the false self gives vent to hostility, which manifests itself as general irritability—an irritation at the same faults in others that we hate in ourselves. Self-hatred always results in some form of self-destructive behavior." (Rabbi's Heartbeat)

The disguise only ends up making things worse as we wonder why we are unable to be our true selves. **Lewis** adds that "God is trying to make you humble so this moment is possible, to take off the silly, ugly, fancy-dress in which we get up and strut around like the little idiots we are." (Mere Christianity)

Our relationship with God is compromised when we are not authentic with others. God has created us in His image. When we try to be someone we are not, we eventually grow to hate our false self. The hatred of the false self leads to a general irritability that seeps out to others.

Maybe you fear taking a risk with a job change because your resources may decline. Maybe you have not shared that new idea with your boss because fear is holding you back.

Do you really wake up every day loving what you do? Do you look forward to the work that consumes your life? Fear prevents change, and thus real freedom, in how we live our lives.

MANNA FROM MULLINS

On the flip side of pride, insecurity can rear its ugly head and prevent us from becoming all we can be for the glory of God. To paraphrase **Rich Mullins** again, we really don't amount to much, and if that's the case then I don't have to be great. If I don't have to be great then I can fail. If I can fail, then that means I tried. And if I try, then we're going to have some fun in the process. Better to try and fail than to not try.

As we know from the life of Abraham Lincoln, failure teaches us to appreciate success. I believe that parents today are trying too hard to protect their children from failure. To some degree I guess this is normal, but sometimes we need to ride the bike without the helmet, chin strap, knee pads, and elbow pads. We need to remember that it's okay to fall - just TRY.

Far too often, as **CS Lewis** states, we settle for trinkets instead of treasure. We forget that the treasure isn't here anyway. But how we seek safety and comfort. We find security in our helmets and padding, although as we grow up our safety net takes on the form of consumption and gain. But all of our false security passes away in the end. None of it fits in our bags upon departure.

Off to climb Chimney Butte. We had no guide, no trail, just what looked like the easy way to go. About a quarter of the way up our intern cut his foot on a rock that fell and cut the back of his heel. He slowed down and decided against the climb so I was on my own (with God). I kept going slowly inching my way up until the wind really picked up in speed and I knew the top was near. I came to a steep point and said 'if this isn't the top, I'm turning back, but I made it over this point and to the top.

Before cresting the butte, I marked a spot with water in the shade to remember my way down. I finally stepped up to the top's surface and was elated, yelling 'I made it', 'I made it'. I took pictures like crazy and then saw the time and knew I had to leave. It was near 8pm Rez time with an hour left. I knew I had to hurry.

I went down and realized immediately that I had gone the wrong way. I came to a landing and looked over the edge and it was sheer cliff. I looked back and saw an uphill climb to go back the way I came up. I went up and felt, this is too much. That way has to be easier. So I came down and looked at the edge—how am I going to get down! This is the wrong way! And panic/fear set in and I had to calm down.

The sun was breaking the horizon at approximately 8:20pm and I knew it would get dark. A sheer edge was not the best choice, so it was uphill again to another route to actually get back down. I remembered the verse 'Do not be afraid, just believe!' **Mark 5:36**. So, up I went facing the fear of being stuck on this butte. I got up and over only to find that I was facing a <u>near</u> sheer edge.

I had just enough landing to go to the edge and see what the drop looked like below. It was near 50 feet straight down until the slope changed enough not to fall. I had to go down face forward (my back against the butte) using my arms and hands as the strongholds.

I was speaking and praying to God the whole way down 'Remember your stronghold', 'Stronghold, stronghold' (some were loose) over and over again (to test the rock). And that Jesus was my cornerstone, our Rock and my salvation! When I made it to where the slope changed and was safe from a fall, I just started praising the Lord and thanking Him for protection.

What a victory in Christ! To overcome that moment of panic/fear by trusting in Him to get me off that mountain—off Chimney Butte before dark. I made it off by 9:30pm. Once was enough in my life.

See what happens when you don't get help from the local Navajos, and in your pride you try to climb a butte that a Navajo man later told me you need ropes to climb? Some younger Navajo teens may disagree, but it was challenging. As I re-read my journal entry from that day, I am reminded of my frailty and weakness. We are in need of a greater stronghold in our life than a rope ladder or bike helmet. We need an unfailing love that will hold us, and all our baggage, together.

The next time you climb a butte in your life, just leave the baggage at the foot of the hill and give the glory to someone greater. Hand the crown to the One who gives you air to breathe and strength to climb the mountain. Find His love and grace at the top of the butte, and be encouraged by the sense of belonging you find in Him. We all yearn for joy and peace, and it is only found in the satisfying love of one person - Jesus Christ.

SCARED TO DEATH – OF OTHERS

Are we living the gospel according to the grace and truth of Christ, as Paul describes in Galatians Chapter 2? Or are we trying to win the approval of men? I think if we were honest, we would admit our tendency to make decisions based on the general consensus of those around us.

Why are we so concerned about what others think of our choices down to the cars we drive and the clothes we wear? Why are material things of such value to us?

> "Look at your life and see how you have filled its emptiness with people. As a result, they have a stranglehold on you. See how they control your behavior by their approval and disapproval. They hold the power to ease your loneliness with their company, to

send your spirits soaring with their praise, to bring you down to the depths with their criticism and rejection. Take a look at yourself spending almost every waking moment of your day placating and pleasing people, whether they are living or dead." (Anthony DeMello, Rabbi's Heartbeat.)

Behavior Trap

We are trying to balance freedom in Christ with the expectations of people, yet we still wonder why we don't live up to others' perceptions. Disapproval is not an option we like in our world. Fear of others becomes something we must fight if we are to actually become the people God made us to be. We feel affirmed when we hear praise, but when the door of criticism opens we fire back out of pride and fear. Perhaps unknowingly, we are daily living to please others.

COURAGEOUS DETERMINATION

I recently went through the pride study with some college students. We discovered that we need determination to just be the very self God has created, to release fear and step out in faith with the courage to be ourselves. Then, we can live a life that pleases God and not man. A new day comes when we wake up excited to do what we love with people we love. Freedom is found when we define who we want to be, rather than looking to others to form our opinion for us. Manning writes in Rabbi's Heartbeat that we must possess "a courageous determination to make unpopular decisions that are expressive of the truth of who we are—not of who we think we should be or who someone else wants us to be."

God is love, and when He defines who we are, we become love as well. That means that we resolve to love both the homeless and the CEO as people. Not as a means to an end, but as the end in itself. Take the mask off and let yourself be His for others, letting go of your false self and your fear of others' disapproval.

SPIRITUAL LOVE VERSUS HUMAN LOVE

We manipulate circumstances or people without stopping to think about how we should act in love toward others and even our family. As you read the quote below by Bonhoeffer, reflect on the extent to which you seek to dominate and coerce others out of selfish motives disguised as love. From the overprotection of our kids, to our relationships with our spouse and friends, how accurately does this describe you?

A spiritual love from the Father brings a beautiful new perspective of grace to our lives, through which we accept others as He sees them. The plank in our eye is removed by God's grace, and we can see others as family. We are, after all, a family with the hope of salvation in the name of Christ.

> "I must release the other person from every attempt of mine to regulate, coerce, and dominate him with my love. I must leave him his freedom to be Christ's; I must meet him only as the person that he already is in Christ's eyes. Spiritual Love—recognizes the true image of the other person which he has received from Jesus Christ. Human love produces human subjection, dependence, constraint; Spiritual love creates Freedom of the brotherhood under the Word." **(**Bonhoeffer, Life Together**)**

We too should have the same image of ourselves as that which Christ has. That image leaves no room for fear. **Richard Foster** adds in Prayer that the "less manipulated we are by the expectations of others, the more open we are to the expectations of God."

Manning has one final quote to top this discussion off: "Here I Am. It's all I got. In humble awareness and sovereign freedom we can truly BE FOR OTHERS without FEAR OF REJECTION or concern for their usefulness to us!"

When Christ is our focus, fear is replaced with His love, grace and truth. His acceptance is greater than any fear imposed by people. We are finally able to stand strong in the very image God has given us, open to His Word and moving toward no opinion of self. His light shines much brighter in your life when you remove the filter of you.

JOSEPH'S PERCEPTION

This is where the judgment of people and circumstances in our lives blind our vision. We perceive things to be bad, like when Joseph was sold into slavery and then thrown into prison despite his integrity. He could have moped around and drowned in a sorrowful woe, but he interpreted the dream and became Pharaoh's right hand man. Joseph removed fear and had the courage to suggest to Pharaoh that a wise man be appointed to discern on behalf of Egypt. He was the man! What a humble response for the Pharaoh (King, like a god) to hand Joseph the reigns of the land, and that his people would submit to Joseph's orders. Pharaoh even said to Joseph in Genesis 41:40, "only with respect to the throne will I be greater than you."

Joseph's perception of his circumstance was positive, believing in his God given ability. That perception enabled Joseph to seize the moment. AND….He was not afraid of HOW he would be PERCEIVED by man or Pharaoh. Amazingly, even when his life seemed to be at its lowest point, Joseph's trust was in God and his desire was to please God alone. May we take a hint from Joseph and keep our focus on Him. That means that we ask first instead of last, "What pleases the Lord?" We are "light in the Lord" according to Ephesians 5:8-10, and we have been told to live as children of light resulting in fruit that consists of all goodness, righteous-ness and truth.

Lord: Today, help me to know I am a beloved child of the Creator, not created to bow to the creatures around us but created to live out love in a peace that reflects your image. May my life be modeled after You, pleasing to the Father **(John 8:29)**.

RAISING ARIZONA AND DEPARTURE

One of the hardest decisions we have had to make as a family was whether to leave the Navajo Reservation. In our life of pride, we want control. We expect our plans to unfold according to our own timing. Trusting God for His provision, living by faith, is not easy. We don't like to accept that we don't have the answers.

But the time had come to leave the Rez and trust God to provide for His ministry in Dilkon. The night we left to head east, a massive thunderstorm with black clouds was coming our way. In almost seven years of being on the field in Dilkon we had never seen a flash flood. That night, the town was struck with such a great rainfall that the old dry creek bed was flowing over guardrails and flooding roads.

Many tears were shed during our last church service, and we felt a sense of loss. Did we go wrong with our decision to leave? What could we have done differently or better while we were there?

The people from the Rez will always be in our hearts, and we will always be in prayer for them. They not only face racism, they are forgotten in their own country even though they were here first.

Talk about pride and living out of fear. Our U.S. Calvary forced the Navajos on an almost 500 mile walk from Arizona to New Mexico during the winter. Many died along the way. This shows the importance of knowledge and action. To paraphrase Manning, intellectual curiosity without courage to act is bankruptcy.

So our full time journey with the Navajo came to an end. There is nothing like living on the Navajo Reservation. It boasts some of the most beautiful country in America, like Canyon De Chelly, now a National Monument, and the town of Dilkon. You should see the sunsets, black silhouettes and color laden skies of the Little Painted Desert with Flagstaff Mountain sixty miles away in the background. Nuzhonia. Beautiful. Rich Mullins knew the beauty of the Rez, as he lived there and visited De Chelly and built hogans for the Navajos. Jesus, the man of no reputation and His mystery are still changing lives for the glory of the Father.

The hardest part of leaving was actually saying goodbye and driving away in the U-Haul truck. We rode in the U-haul while our dog was in the back of the Jeep on the trailer. Navajo style. In all seriousness, the Navajo people, or the Dine, are an amazing tribe. They are so soft hearted and welcoming of the bilagana, or white man, despite the past. A local man once told me some members of the community were in tears as they watched the trading post in the old West transform into a brand new grocery store in town. They are true forerunners as they slept on sheep-skins in hogans on dirt floors. Some still live this way, life unadulterated with no running water or electricity. But content nonetheless. We really don't need much do we?

The last message I preached on the Rez was entitled "Love Let's Go and LOVE, LETS GO!" As Rob Bell notes in his Nooma video "Dust," we must believe, trust and know that the disciples are capable. Jesus left his disciples to tell the world about Him, and He still uses ragamuffins like us to share His unfailing love.

We truly do have to LET GO of our pride to love and trust God. He is in control. Jesus' love let go. Even of his own life on earth, obedient to death on a cross for the joy set before Him.

LOVE, let's go! It's time to move on and out of the walls of the church building so that an unbelieving world can see an imitation of Christ that is alive with servanthood and caring for those in need. How else will we know the least of these if we are not WITH them. Or, just maybe, I am the least of these.

CHAPTER 8

FROM PRIDE TO LIVING OUT LOVE

COMPLETING THE WORSHIP CIRCLE

I was diligently working as always in the enshrined cubicle and God was whispering to pick up this book by Tim Hughes titled "Here I Am to Worship." As I began reading I was struck with the most amazing quote combining worship and missiology. Check this out:

> *"WORSHIP WITHOUT MISSION IS SELF-INDULGENT
> MISSION WITHOUT WORSHIP IS SELF-DEFEATING"*
> —Bishop Graham Bell

Stop and think of the implications of this message. In our worship we must include the call to make disciples among the nations. We do a fine job of raising our hands in "worship," singing along with our favorite Christian artists, fellowship, and perhaps taking the sacraments depending on your church. But are we completing the worship circle?

Have we become self-indulgent in our worship? Is it all about hearing a nice worship set and heading off to work or to get the latte, missing our suffering neighbors on the way? Does mission follow our praise of God, giving of ourselves in thanksgiving, or better quoted in <u>Rich Christians in an age of Hunger</u>, will we "simplify our lives so the poor can simply live?"

Church, are we completing the worship circle? When we do serve, are we including the worship and name of Christ in the work? If not, our mission is self-defeating.

JONATHAN EDWARDS:
HEAT IN THE HEART AND LIGHT IN THE MIND

Jonathan Edwards describes it best this way:

> "There is no more heat in the heart than there is light in the mind and no more heat than what is justified by the light."

We get all excited and worship with zeal, and maybe crowd surf, with our favorite artist. The heat is in the heart, but what should really move us is the light in the mind, the Word of God! Don't get me wrong, I play enough chords to be dangerous and I love music and the heat. But do not make the mistake of forgetting that the Light of the Word is your foundation. And then take the next step and transfer that light into your community. Allow yourself to be a living sacrifice to be used by God for the salvation of the world.

We see Christ on the cross from the Word, but how will the world see Jesus if not by our lives? It means we daily take up our cross in servant-hood and reach out to our community. We go into the streets to draw people to the cross of Christ. Perhaps that's what Christ meant when He said to carry your cross to find and live your passion for His glory. By His Word and grace, the truth will be told as Christ Himself testified to Pilate was the reason for His coming to earth.

It is time we testify to the truth by our actions, as 1 John 3:18 says.

WORSHIP BUZZ

Remember, worship without mission is self-indulgent. Rich Mullins said it best. He must have been a prophet used by God. Mullins said that sound doctrine is better any day than goose bumps from the buzz. Some will church shop based on how they feel and on the production of music alone. Does the worship feature choruses or hymns? To each his own, yes, but as Edwards wrote years before our time, may there be "no more heat than what is justified by the light!"

COLOSSIANS 3

An amazing passage that sums up our study comes from **Colossians 3** as this new self continues to grow daily in the immersion of Christ. We begin to put off all the old habits as we recognize pride in our lives from the idols of the world: lust, sexual immorality, anger and filthy language.

In **verse 10** we see the meat of this passage, which gives us encourage-ment in our battle with pride. We find that we are "renewed in the knowl-edge in the image of its Creator." Do you see the significance in that text?

101

C.S. Lewis writes that we need to "be reminded more than instructed." The new creation is being renewed in His image. We are truly loved by God, beautiful as we are. In Him we find radical self-acceptance, and we can be thankful for how He has made us - children of God to serve and do His will. A freedom ensues in our lives as we embrace this renewed knowledge knowing that as God's chosen people, "dearly loved," we can clothe ourselves with "compassion, kindness, humility, gentleness and patience."

Do you see it coming together now? As we forgive one another, the scales of pride fall off and we accept one another because Christ is all and is in all. "And over all these virtues" the last thing we put on is love. The new graces that take the place of pride in our lives create a love that is sincere, from Romans 12:9, and love binds the virtues together in perfect unity.

Peace takes hold in our lives and we let the Word of God "dwell in us richly," as we see in Colossians 3:16, teaching and sharing with thanksgiving and praise. We become unafraid of what others think and we dance in our underwear like David - although not so much in public. Without pride, we are full of joy again and we let go of self once and for all in the name of the Lord, giving thanks to the Father.

ROMANS 12 AND LIVING OUT LOVE

John Piper writes in <u>Desiring God</u> that "love is the overflow of joy in God that gladly meets the needs of others." This overflow of joy in God is expressed through an outpouring of love that gladly meets the needs of others. Our focus on self, whether all or woe, is now replaced by a love for Christ and really knowing Him. Love takes us to the feet of others.

Look at Romans 12:9-20. Love must be sincere. Sincere means free of hypocrisy. It is time we live this out, let our yes be yes and our no be no. Have the integrity to do what we believe. Put our very self and lives next to the poor. Remember what Paul wrote in 1 Thessalonians 2:8 – we are called to not only bring the gospel, but our very lives.

David Bosch wrote in <u>Transforming Mission</u> that "the church needs the poor to stay close to God." I'm not a fan of this dichotomy of us versus them, or the haves and have nots, but we must know our own position and realize that there are marginalized people in society who suffer. That perspective should lead us to act out of humility, to come alongside the less fortunate and listen to their hearts, to learn their story like Christ when He was with the Samaritan woman at the well.

As Galatians 5:6 says, the only thing that counts is faith expressing itself through love. The Church must be devoted to one another in brotherly love, serving with a spiritual fervor. We make time for real communion and prayer with God, and we share with God's people who are in need. As we recognize our pride and remove it from our lives, we are willing to associate with people of "low" position or to do "menial" work.

Like Mother Teresa, we can honor our brothers and bring them dignity and respect simply by caring about their lives. Real success in life is found in serving others and caring for the hungry and naked. We take literally the command to not be conceited, and with a contrite heart we love much. Be blessed to give your lives away and run the race with all your strength.

SECRET OF CONTENTMENT

After we submit to God and His Word and worship Him with an active love response, we can finally rest in an area that I believe is crucial to our spiritual growth. Paul writes in Philippians that he knows what it is to be in need, and he knows what it is to have plenty. He writes that he has learned the secret of being content in any and every situation, whether well fed or hungry, whether living in plenty or in want. (Philippians 4:12) This is huge if you take some time to grasp what Paul is writing. It is time to stop yearning for more and more. The toys of this world will pass away, and these idols that can become their own false mini-gods present a danger to our life of worship. We should see by now that the only radical love affair worth chasing is Jesus Christ.

CREATOR VS. CREATURES

Stop loving the creatures – from cars, money or men and women - and set your eyes on what is unseen. Worship instead the great Creator of all things. The radical love affair is alive and well as He is a jealous God and wants our affection to be for Him. As we seek first His Kingdom then all these are added to us being in a right relationship with Him.

Don't get me wrong. We will struggle because we are in a fight against not flesh and blood but real principalities of darkness. We fight daily in this communion with God to make conscious choices that say no to all the lust and allure on television. We choose to live a life that is worthy of the calling that our life is now hidden in Christ. It is so important to the continuation of the Gospel that we model integrity to children and teens in our culture. The contentment that brings the peace that the world is seeking comes from the Holy Spirit whispering through His Word that *"I AM."* He is enough!

I can do all things through His strength, including letting go of pride and trusting that His grace is sufficient. I am content, wholly and fully, created and renewed in the image of the Creator.

COURAGE TO ACCEPT

I think that when most of us think of faith, we think of trust or belief in something we cannot see or understand with our finite minds. God's Word tells us that faith is being sure of what we hope for and certain of what we do not see. This is what the ancients were commended for in Hebrews 11: 1-2. As we have studied the pride in our lives, though, I have come across a definition of faith that relates to trust from a different perspective. Tillich writes that "faith is the courage to accept that you are accepted by God."

The courage to accept that you are accepted by God. I can trust in Him for who he has made me to be in His image, realizing that I am beloved by God the Father. Indeed, He sent His Son as an atoning sacrifice for my sins. This hope is one that is assured, and as a result I step out in faith with courage to capture His grace, receiving something I don't deserve. I am equipped to love God and others.

I understand now that acceptance comes from Christ, not the world and its trinkets. I am an heir of Christ and He calls me His friend. In response, I am compelled to answer Jesus' call to love others. In this new courage to

104

accept His hand and grace, may we bear fruit as we obey the command to love each other, especially by doing good to the family of believers.

A LOVE BEYOND SELF

Our lives should reflect the faith of the Thessalonians. Lets take a look at the passage from the first chapter of Thessalonians, verse four. "For we know, brothers loved by God, that He has chosen you, because our gospel came to you not simply with words, but also with power with the Holy Spirit and with deep conviction." Stop there for a moment and look at this story.

We are chosen by God, the author and perfecter of our faith, to be loved by Him. The gospel was delivered to the people of Thessalonica not just with words, but also with power and deep conviction. If they were convicted, it was because they saw something that was real, alive and in action for the glory of God and the sake of the gospel. They witnessed the love of Christ, and in the same verse we read that they knew how Paul lived among them *for their sake.*

PATIENT IMPATIENCE

As a result, the Thessalonians became imitators of Christ, and despite their suffering they welcomed the message with joy. Does this describe us today as believers? If we don't feel well, do we make it to church? The Thessalonians became a model to all the believers around them and the Lord's message rang out across the land because of the action that was borne of their faith. Does the world know our faith by our lives? Is our faith in motion serving the living and true God in the "patient impatience" of waiting for His Son?

David Bosch wrote in <u>Transforming Mission</u> that "since God's victory is certain, believers can work both patiently and enthusiastically, blending careful planning with urgent obedience, motivated by the **patient impatience** of the Christian hope." The time to die daily and love beyond ourselves for His glory is now. Get close to others' needs, hear their story, and find the grace to express your faith in love with a servant's mindset. Imitate Christ with the intent to love God and your neighbor.

THE CHRIST WALK IS BEAUTY

The journey of finding God and enjoying His presence continues in my own life. I recently went back to Canyon De Chelly on the Rez. It is a place where you can see His creation and His greatness, and our "big selves" diminish as we fall into His arms and breathe in His beauty. The Navajo have an expression that essentially equates to Walk in Beauty. There is a special harmony in seeing and feeling the presence of God as we sit with Him in the grandeur and beauty of His creation, in awe of His love for me, a child beloved by God the Father. We really cannot fathom His greatness or encompass His love that is so free. May the grace that is in our hearts be evident to the world.

May we become a living sacrifice, holy and pleasing to God, as we live out faith expressed in love. Christ took sacrificial action and healed when He was near those in need. How will we know the poor if we are not close to them? David didn't want to offer a sacrifice that cost him nothing. The Walk in Beauty truly releases self to love, forgive and accept people in the image of Christ.

BIRTH PANGS AND LOVE MUCH®

As our time with the Navajo drew to a close, my heart was convicted by the AIDS crisis and whether the church was actually searching for intervention solutions. As time progressed, through much prayer and time alone with God out on the buttes of Dilkon coupled with fasting, we arrived at our new ministry. The name is the Neighborhood Engagement, Love Much®. We are forming teams that essentially adopt suffering neighborhoods locally, nationally and overseas to search for sustainment solutions.

Our mantra, one I believe Christ modeled with the Samaritan woman at the well and again with Zachariah, is to listen and learn, having a love much response. Jesus listened to the woman, he was hanging out on Zachariah's turf, and he met their needs. The love much response for our ministry comes from Luke 7:47, where the sinful woman anoints Jesus' feet and He declares that she is forgiven much and thus loved much. She met his most simple needs by wetting his feet with her tears, wiping them with her hair, and then kissing and anointing Him with perfume. In verse fifty, we learn that she was saved as a result of her faith.

You see, in the end we have to beware daily to not be the Pharisee in our pride, but instead to love much in our faithful relationship with God and others. Perhaps now we can see others and their needs as we recognize the effects of our pride, let go of our self, and die everyday to the flesh in this mystery of grace. We too declare our brokenness and with a heart of humility that is made alive in Christ, we love the Lord our God with all of our heart, mind, soul and strength.

We truly love others, and love forces us to ask the same question on this journey from pride to love that was asked of Jesus Himself,

Who is my neighbor?

ONE MORE SHOUT FROM THE HEART

The recognition of pride in my life has allowed me to triumph over the arrogance that once masked the excuse of ignorance. Worshipping God and knowing his Son, Jesus Christ, is the only path to love, joy and peace in this world. Our circumstances and pride are covered by the grace and truth of His Word, and encouragement rolls in to refresh the saints and restore hope to our fellow man.

May our hearts and the passion of our lives beat for the declaration of His name among the nations as we become servant minded sacrificial Kingdom builders for the glory and splendor of His holiness.

Church, Body of Christ, World, let go of your pride that keeps you from drawing closer to God the Father, Son and Holy Spirit.

When we die to self to live and worship our risen Savior, Jesus Christ, we find freedom and joy.

Galatians 5:6 says that "the only thing that counts is faith expressing itself through love."

Now, go live out this love.

HOMELESS HAPPENINGS

I sit here at 'Bluegrass Inn' in downtown Nashville in the fall of '05 attending the National Youth Workers Convention listening to live music by Gypsy. A young Jack Carter has a Martin and a McPherson guitar and is a wicked acoustic guitar player like he's on fire. They have a label and in some way I feel at ease, comfortable.

TEAR IN MY BEER (NOT REALLY)

I was walking the strip and noticed a man playing guitar so I put on my eight dollar silver chromed Elvis glasses (a proud purchase) and just leaned in against the brick wall listening to his songs. The passerby youth leaders just gazed at Elvis and sounds of Cash, Haggard and the like.

This sweet little melody touched my ears as I am not a fan of country music although from Texas and it rang out something like this that day. 'There's a tear in my beer and I'm crying for you dear'…I was like 'man that is a great little sound.' 'Did you write that song' and he chuckled and informed me of a more famous name and that he was homeless.

I took Art to lunch that day and now I know why the world dislikes the church. We think or look as though we have it all figured out and we fall short. An air of haughtiness rested over our shoulders that day as we waited in a packed line of believers as Art waited in line with his guitar.

Its amazing that people are hurting and need help and Art shared how he lived under a tent around the corner. Where are we church? How are we really being and doing? 'God help us all and have mercy on us that we would humble ourselves before you do!!'-

'May we remove self in order to see a love greater than ourselves that captures the heart of the world engaging imaginations to better the future to leave our mark of grace and truth for the glory of Jesus name and Kingdom .'—Fall of 2005 journal entry

2 Peter 3:18 But grow in the grace and knowledge of our Lord and Savior Jesus Christ. To Him be glory both now and forever. Amen.

STORAGE CLOSET FRIENDS

My experience at the local homeless shelter in Louisville has consisted of reaching out to men and women in the kitchen where we distribute food and also towels and toiletries. This ministry is unique in that it has a mailing address for homeless men and women who are trying to get a job and make ends meet to get off the streets.

After breakfast I work in the storage closet which allows people to leave up to two bags in the closet where they can shower and then go out and dress up for a job interview. The bags are tagged for a one month use and then re-issued if they stay longer or need more time to store their belongings.

Amazing how God works when you are sitting in the closet to serve others and you get this perspective and insight from a man at the shelter. I just casually asked him as he returned his bag what his plans were for the day and he told me that he would be sitting with cancer patients who have no family. He had undergone chemotherapy himself and was grateful to survive cancer and made this choice to encourage others.

He also passed out questionnaires to earn a living walking around town asking others about being a bone marrow donor. What a journey in our pride as we think we might be sacrificing our time or is this worth the trouble or effort. Am I enabling these folks,..

was Jesus?

BRIEF NOTE ON RACISM AND AIDS CRISIS

Boy, this is a tough subject that really no one wants to write or read about or directly actively reconcile. But in our pride, maybe that's the problem. A recent Dr. from Ghana just recently mentioned to me that we are shades of brown. What a shame that we have made this a black and white world. I believe all of us are guilty. Guilty of being afraid of what others might think of our behavior.

Otherwise, it seems that we would love, share and inhabit more than we currently do with people that might be a little out of our culture or should we admit honestly 'out of our league'. Pride really is an amazing trick Satan uses to separate and destroy people. Whether after reading this material you agree or not, we live out of pride, everyday. It's really just a matter of how we balance our act and really live out love to a hurting world. God help us and give us strength to really accept and embrace all cultures and people created in the image of God.

Isn't that really what it comes down to as we 'perceive our reality'? The truth is we are all created in His image and valuable to the creator. And yet, as Bono declares in Rolling Stone magazine a latent racism, in regard to the action taken in the AIDS crisis. What keeps us from moving toward actively making a difference? Our pride of self-absorption and inward focus which only stimulates apathy. World Vision cites the number one reason that people don't respond in the AIDS crisis is that 'it doesn't affect us'.

Oh my, does it ever affect the loudness of the truth we live as followers of Christ. As the church in America, are we actually going to sit idly by and just keep listening to the stats of broken lives and children by a disease that is treatable and preventable? What does David declare about the sacrifices of God from the Psalms in 51? 'The sacrifices of God are a broken and contrite heart.

Man, apparently we are not as close to the heart of God as we think, if ours does not lean on the brokenhearted and crushed in spirit from AIDS or any hindrance. Did you know that every 10 minutes someone in America is infected with AIDS. Lookout and be careful, because AIDS, like Christ is no respecter of persons. Think of the homeless, are we there? Drug addicts, is the Body there? Just some things in our pride to start taking notice because the world notices our movement.

COMPASSION PERMANENCE

Pg.39 Good News about Injustice
This is absolutely necessary for this book as we must truly begin to align our convictions to compassion permanence. Gary Haugen in **Good News About Injustice** declares that this permanence is a *'courageous and*

111

generous capacity to remember the needs of an unjust world even when they are out of our immediate sight.'

CONSISTENT COMMUNICATION

After the short-term mission trip, which needs to be redefined with intention upon completion, we return from the experience of being in Africa or with the Navajo. We forget though after being 'on fire' for a month that the grind of life returns and we simply forget. Compassion permanence must be retained through consistent communication with our partners through technology. Our partners need access to email and computers to really share the story of how the Body of Christ lives and struggles to daily serve Christ.

I believe the church at large is failing in regard to this method of really employing strong advocates that will return from serving together to retain compassion hearing the story of the saints and faithfully loving our neighbors.

The injustice in Africa, even in our own backyard, we do not see, but we must trust God and take our conviction to commitment and perhaps as Americans grant opportunity to those who don't have the resources for growth. Whether it is access to medicine or education or freed from bonded labor or prostitution, as blessed Americans we must find our cause God has given us purpose for and claim it for His glory and then take action.

Make the effort to directly support a location by traveling to and adopting a need or support a foundation you believe in or your churches' local projects in your own communities. Do something outside of self. We are so selfish and continue to want more and more. Have mercy Lord on our comfort.

Help us to get out of the house and help others. Why do we stress over careers and success and money and forget to manage our own home **(1 Tim. 3:5)** or not make time for our children who are only around for such a short time. May we see with your eyes and heart and realize once and for all what is important. And as believers, we are not perfect and fail at this very thing. We can easily get so out of focus on what really matters to God.

The very fast He chooses is not for us to humble ourselves for a day, but to loose the chains of injustice, set the oppressed free and share our food with the hungry, providing shelter to the wanderer. Oh God, what have we done out of our fear we live in but just the opposite of His fast, as we drive by the homeless guy asking for money at the freeway exit as we judge his motives and assume he's drunk or on drugs. We just miss the point of Christ's message to love one another in our hurried schedules.

Richard Foster writes in **Prayer** that *Jesus' life was lived in an unhurried peace.* No worries. I'll get there Mary and Martha for Lazarus. Just be patient and trust. That's also part of the problem. We don't want to wait for anything in America. Drive-thru fast food chains are not fast enough, or your email, Internet downloads, traffic, etc. We are so spoiled by our own culture and we want what we want NOW! (Will this book ever end, etc.)

Okay, I'll breathe now and let you rest from the rant. Lord help us to be others minded in a 'me' world. Just for a moment....